PRESERVE TH<

Seasonal Canning from Garden to Table

Mary R. Williams

Copyright © 2025 by Mary R. Williams

All rights reserved. No part of this book may be reproduced, stored in a retrieval system, or transmitted in any form or by any means—electronic, mechanical, photocopying, recording, or otherwise—without the prior written permission of the publisher, except for brief quotations used in reviews, articles, or scholarly works.

Table of Contents

Mary R. Williams
Table of Contents
Introduction
    What is Canning?
    History of Home Canning
    Safety First: Understanding Botulism and Food Safety
    Overview of Canning Methods
Chapter 1: Getting Started with Canning
    Types of Canning: Water Bath vs. Pressure Canning
    Essential Equipment and Tools
    Understanding Acidity and pH in Canning
    Jar Types, Sizes, and Lid Systems
Chapter 2: Preparing for Success
    Sterilizing Jars and Equipment
    Preparing Your Workspace
    Choosing the Right Recipes
    Understanding Headspace, Processing Times, and Altitude Adjustments
Chapter 3: Water Bath Canning
    High-Acid Foods Explained
    Step-by-Step Water Bath Canning Process
    Troubleshooting Water Bath Issues
Chapter 4: Pressure Canning
    Low-Acid Foods and the Need for Pressure
    Types of Pressure Canners
    Step-by-Step Pressure Canning Process
    Safety Tips and Common Mistakes

Chapter 5: Canning Recipes – Fruits & Jams
- Whole and Sliced Fruits in Syrup
- Classic and Low-Sugar Jams
- Marmalades, Jellies, and Fruit Butters
- Pie Fillings and Compotes

Chapter 6: Canning Recipes – Vegetables & Pickles
- Pickled Vegetables (Cucumbers, Beets, Carrots)
- Relishes and Chutneys
- Tomatoes, Sauces, and Salsa (Water Bath and Pressure Variants)
- Green Beans, Corn, and Mixed Vegetables (Pressure Canning)

Chapter 7: Canning Recipes – Meats & Meals
- Canning Poultry, Beef, and Pork
- Soups, Stews, and Chili
- Beans and Legumes
- Bone Broth and Stocks

Chapter 8: Troubleshooting & Tips
- Identifying Seal Failures
- Reprocessing Guidelines
- Storage and Shelf Life
- Common Questions Answered

Chapter 9: Creative Canning & Gifting
- Unique Flavor Combinations
- Labeling and Decorating Jars
- Creating Gift Sets and Seasonal Baskets

Introduction

What is Canning?

Anning is a method of preserving food in which the food is processed and sealed in airtight containers (usually glass jars or metal cans). This technique extends the shelf life of food by preventing the growth of microorganisms that cause spoilage.

How to Use Canning: Depending on the kind, food is prepared by being cleaned, peeled, chopped, or cooked. Packing: The food is placed into jars or cans, often with a liquid like syrup, brine, or water.

Sealing: Containers are sealed with lids.

Processing: To kill harmful yeasts, molds, and bacteria, the sealed containers are heated for a specific amount of time to a particular temperature. Water bath canning: For high-acid foods like fruits, pickles, and jams.

Pressure canning: This method is used to safely kill Clostridium botulinum spores in low-acid foods like vegetables, meat, and soups at higher temperatures. Cooling and Storage: After processing, jars cool and form a vacuum seal. Properly canned foods can last 1–5 years or longer if stored in a cool, dark place.

Benefits of Canning:

Long shelf life

No need for refrigeration

conserves seasonal produce control over the ingredients, such as sugar, salt, and preservatives

History of Home Canning

Home canning dates back more than two centuries and is closely related to the development of food preservation techniques. Here's a concise overview:

1. Canning's history (late 1700s–early 1800s) 1795 – Napoleonic Challenge: Napoleon Bonaparte offered a reward to anyone who could devise a reliable method to preserve food for his armies.

1809 – Nicolas Appert's Method: A French confectioner and brewer, Appert developed a process of sealing food in glass jars and heating them. This was the birth of canning.

1810: The use of tin-coated iron cans was patented by Englishman Peter Durand, making the method more durable for commercial and military use. 2. Spread to America (Mid-1800s)

Canning reached the U.S. in the early 1800s, initially as a commercial process.

Home canning began to gain popularity by the 1850s, particularly with the availability of Mason jars, which John Landis Mason patented in 1858. These jars had a threaded top and reusable lid, making home preservation more practical and safe.

3. Safety and pressure canning in the early 20th century Botulism concerns emerged as people tried to can low-acid foods (meat, vegetables).

1920s – Pressure Canners: Developed to reach the higher temperatures needed to safely preserve low-acid foods and kill Clostridium botulinum spores.

Ball Corporation (founded in 1880) became a leading supplier of canning jars and promoted home canning through booklets and manuals.

4. WWII and Post-War Era

During World War II, home canning surged as part of the "Victory Garden" movement. Families were encouraged to grow and preserve their food to support the war effort.

Home canning declined after the war due to technological advancements and the rise of supermarkets, despite its continued popularity in rural areas. 5. Modern Era (1970s – Present)

1970s revival: Driven by the back-to-the-land movement, environmental awareness, and rising food prices.

The National Center for Home Food Preservation (NCHFP) and the United States Department of Agriculture (USDA) provided the most recent safety guidelines and recipes based on research. Today, home canning is enjoying a resurgence due to:

Interest in self-reliance, organic/local foods, emergency preparedness, and homesteading.

The craft food movement, where small-batch jams, pickles, and sauces are popular.

Safety First: Understanding Botulism and Food Safety

Here's a concise and informative guide titled "Safety First: Understanding Botulism and Food Safety in Canning" that covers the key points you need to know:

Understanding Botulism and Food Safety in Canning: Safety First Is botulism a disease? Botulism is a rare but potentially fatal illness caused by a toxin produced by Clostridium botulinum bacteria. These bacteria thrive in low-oxygen, low-acid environments — like improperly canned foods — and can produce a neurotoxin that affects the nervous system, potentially causing paralysis or death.

Why is Botulism a Concern in Canning?

Home-canned foods, especially low-acid items like vegetables, meats, and soups, are at risk because they create ideal conditions for C. botulinum if not processed correctly. The spores of this bacterium can survive boiling water temperatures, so more rigorous methods are required.

Types of Foods at Risk

Low-acid foods (pH above 4.6): Green beans, corn, meats, poultry, seafood, potatoes

Medium-acid foods: Tomatoes (must often be acidified before water bath canning)

High-acid foods: Fruits, jams, jellies, pickles (lower risk when canned properly)

Safe Methods of Canning 1. Canning under pressure (for low-acid foods) is Necessary for foods with a pH above 4.6.

Reaches 240–250°F (116–121°C), enough to kill C. botulinum spores.

Use a tested and approved pressure canning recipe (from USDA or university extensions).

2. Water Bath Canning (for high-acid foods)

Suitable for jams, jellies, pickles, and fruits.

Boiling water (212°F or 100°C) is sufficient due to the high acidity.

Key Safety Tips

Use tested recipes from trusted sources (e.g., USDA, Ball, National Center for Home Food Preservation).

Never alter acid, sugar, or processing time in recipes.

Always use clean, sterilized jars and new lids.

After 12 to 24 hours, check the jar seals. Unrefrigerated storage of a broken seal is not recommended. Store in a cool, dark place, and label with date.

Signs of Botulism in Canned Foods

Bulging lids

Leaking or rusting jars

Unusual or foul odor when opened Foam or bubbles in the liquid

Food discoloration or mold

If in doubt, throw it out! Do not taste food to test safety.

What to Do if You Suspect Contamination

Do not open suspect jars indoors.

Wrap the jar in plastic and dispose of it according to local hazardous waste guidelines.

If already opened and suspect, wear gloves and sanitize surfaces thoroughly.

Final Thoughts

Canning is a fantastic way to preserve food, but safety must always come first. With the right equipment, tested recipes, and careful attention to detail, you can enjoy the rewards of home canning without the risks.

Overview of Canning Methods

The most common canning techniques, their workings, and the foods they work best with are outlined in the following overview: 1. Water Bath Canning

What It Is:

A method where jars are submerged in boiling water (212°F / 100°C) for a specified time.

Best For:

High-acid foods (pH ≤ 4.6), which naturally inhibit harmful bacteria.

Fruits (peaches, berries, apples)

Jams, jellies, fruit butters

Tomatoes (with added acid like lemon juice)

relishes and pickles Pros:

Simple and inexpensive equipment

Great for beginners

Cons:

Not safe for low-acid foods

Process times that are longer than those for pressure canning 2. Canning under pressure What It Is:

Clostridium botulinum spores are eradicated by processing the jars in a sealed pressure canner at temperatures of 240–250°F (116–121°C). Best For:

Low-acid foods (pH > 4.6)

Poultry and meat Seafood

Vegetables (green beans, corn, carrots)

Legumes

Stews and soups made without flour or cornstarch as a thickener Pros:

Safe for all food types

High-heat, quick processing Cons:

Requires special equipment

Slight learning curve

3. Steam Canning

What It Is:

Uses steam in a closed vessel to reach 212°F (100°C), which is the same temperature as a boiling water bath. Best For:

Same as water bath canning (high-acid foods only)

Pros:

Uses less water

Accelerates healing Cons:

unsafe for foods low in acid May need adjustments for altitude

4. Atmospheric Steam Canning (Electric Steam Canners)

What It Is:

A newer method using electric steam canners with temperature and time controls for high-acid foods.

Best For:

Jams, jellies, fruits, and pickles

Pros:

User-friendly

More compact than water bath setups

Cons:

Limited capacity

Not for low-acid foods

Important Safety Tips:

Always use tested recipes from trusted sources (e.g., USDA, Ball, National Center for Home Food Preservation).

Adjust for altitude: Higher elevations require longer processing times or more pressure.

Inspect jars for cracks, use new lids, and test seals after cooling.

Chapter 1: Getting Started with Canning

Types of Canning: Water Bath vs. Pressure Canning

Here's a clear comparison of Water Bath Canning vs. Pressure Canning:

Canning in a Water Bath Uses: High-acid foods (pH below 4.6), like fruits, jams, jellies, pickles, and acidic tomatoes (with added acid).

Jars are immersed for a predetermined amount of time in boiling water (212°F / 100°C). Equipment: Large pot with a rack to keep jars off the bottom.

Why: The high acidity prevents the growth of harmful bacteria, so boiling water is enough to safely preserve the food.

Limitations: Cannot safely process low-acid foods (vegetables, meats, poultry, seafood).

Canning under pressure Uses: Low-acid foods (pH above 4.6), such as vegetables, meats, poultry, seafood, and some low-acid tomato products.

Process: Jars are processed in a sealed pressure canner where steam pressure raises the temperature to 240-250°F (116-121°C), killing heat-resistant bacteria like Clostridium botulinum.

Equipment: Pressure canner (not a pressure cooker) with a locking lid, pressure gauge, and vent.

Why? Because bacteria spores cannot be destroyed by boiling water alone without a higher temperature. Limitations: More complex equipment and process; must follow exact pressure and timing guidelines.

Table of Contents Feature Water Bath Canning Pressure Canning

Suitable Foods High-acid (fruits, jams, pickles) Low-acid (vegetables, meats)

Temperature Boiling water (212°F / 100°C) Steam under pressure (240-250°F)

Equipment Boiling water canner or pot Pressure canner

Safety Concern Acid prevents bacteria growth and Kills heat-resistant bacteria spores

Processing Time Usually longer Usually shorter

I'll break down step-by-step instructions for both Water Bath Canning and Pressure Canning so you can get started safely.

Water Bath Canning: Step-by-Step

What you require: Canner or deep stockpot: large pot with lid Rack for canning (to keep jars off the floor) Mason jars with lids and screw bands

Jar lifter or tongs

Clean towels

Funnel, bubble remover, and lid lifter tools (optional but helpful)

Steps:

Prepare jars and lids:

Wash jars and lids in hot, soapy water. Well, rinse. Keep jars warm (in simmering water or a warm oven) to prevent cracking when filled.

Lids should be warmed in hot (not boiling) water to soften the sealing compound.

Prepare your food:

Follow a tested recipe for your specific food.

Fill jars with prepared food using a funnel, leaving recommended headspace (usually 1/4 to 1/2 inch).

Remove air bubbles:

Use a plastic or wooden spatula to slide around inside the jar and release trapped air.

Clean jar rims:

Wipe rims with a clean damp cloth to ensure a good seal.

Apply lids and screw bands:

Place lids on jars and screw bands finger-tight (not too tight).

Place jars in canner:

Put jars on a rack in the boiling water canner.

Water should cover jars by at least 1 inch.

Process jars:

Bring water to a full rolling boil.

Start timing according to your recipe (processing time depends on food and jar size).

Throughout the process, keep the water boiling. Remove jars:

Use a jar lifter to remove jars carefully.

Place jars on a towel or rack to cool undisturbed for 12-24 hours.

Verify seals: Test lids by pressing the center after cooling. They should be concave and not pop.

Remove screw bands, wipe jars, label, and store.

Pressure Canning: Step-by-Step

What you need:

Pressure canner (with a pressure gauge or weighted gauge)

lids for mason jars with screw bands Jar lifter, funnel, bubble remover, lid lifter

Clean towels

Steps:

Get the lids and jars ready: Similar to water bath canning (wash, rinse, warm lids, and keep jars warm). Food preparation: Follow a tested low-acid recipe.

Fill jars with food, leaving proper headspace (usually 1 to 1.25 inches).

Remove air bubbles and clean rims:

Same as a water bath.

Apply lids and screw bands:

Same as a water bath.

Put the jars in the pressure cooker: Place jars on a rack inside canner.

The canner's bottom should be filled with the recommended amount of water—usually two to three inches. Seal the canner:

Close the lid securely.

Leave the vent open and heat on high until steam flows steadily for 10 minutes to purge air.

Build pressure:

Close the vent or place weight on the vent to start pressure buildup.

Bring pressure to the required level (e.g., 10, 11, or 15 psi depending on altitude and recipe).

Start timing:

When pressure is reached, begin processing time.

Keep the pressure constant throughout. Depressurize canner:

Turn off the heat and let pressure drop naturally (don't force it).

Wait until the pressure gauge reads zero and no steam escapes before opening.

Remove jars:

Carefully open the lid away from you.

Use a jar lifter to remove jars.

Place jars on a towel or rack to cool undisturbed.

Check seals:

Similar to a water bath.

Essential Equipment and Tools

Here's a clear list of essential equipment and tools you'll need for canning safely and effectively:

1. Canning Jars

Mason jars or other heat-safe glass jars designed for canning

Sizes vary (pints, quarts, half-pints)

2. Lids and Bands

lids in two pieces (flat lids with metal screw bands and sealing compound) Use new lids each time; bands can be reused if undamaged

3. Large Pot or Water Bath Canner

For high-acid foods (fruits, pickles, jams)

A deep pot with a rack to keep jars off the bottom

4. Pressure Canner

Needed for low-acid foods (vegetables, meats, soups)

provides the higher temperatures needed to kill spores of botulism and other bacteria 5. Jar Lifter

Tongs made specifically to safely remove hot jars from boiling water 6. Funnel

Wide-mouth funnel to fill jars without spilling

7. Bubble Remover / Headspace Tool

Plastic or silicone tool to remove air bubbles and measure proper headspace in jars

8. Lid Lifter / Magnetic Tool

Magnetized tool to lift lids out of hot water without touching them

9. Clean Towels or Cloths

to clean the rims of jars before sealing and drying them 10. Timer

To keep track of processing times precisely

11. Canning Rack or Cooling Rack

To hold jars upright during processing and to cool after canning

Understanding Acidity and pH in Canning

A concise explanation of the significance of pH and acidity in canning can be found here: Understanding Acidity and pH in Canning

1. What is pH?

On a scale from 0 to 14, pH measures a substance's acidity or basicity. pH 7 is neutral, pH 0 is acidic, and pH 7 or higher is basic (alkaline). 2. Why Acidity Matters in Canning

Acidity affects the safety and shelf life of canned foods.

High-acid foods (pH ≤ 4.6) inhibit the growth of harmful bacteria like Clostridium botulinum (which causes botulism).

If not properly processed, foods with low acidity (pH greater than 4.6) may encourage bacterial growth. 3. Categories of Foods Based on Acidity

High-acid foods: fruits, tomatoes (usually acidic but sometimes borderline), pickles, sauerkraut, jams, jellies.

Low-acid foods: vegetables (green beans, corn), meats, poultry, seafood, soups.

4. Canning Methods Based on Acidity

Water bath canning is safe only for high-acid foods because the acid prevents bacterial growth.

Pressure canning is required for low-acid foods to reach higher temperatures (240°F or 116°C) that kill spores of Clostridium botulinum.

5. Changing the pH for Safe Canning When canning borderline acidic foods (like tomatoes), acid is often added (lemon juice or vinegar) to lower the pH below 4.6.

Commercial vinegar and bottled lemon juice have standardized acidity, which is important for safety.

6. Assessing pH test strips or meters can help measure acidity, but for home canning, it's best to follow trusted recipes and guidelines rather than experimenting with pH on your own.

7. Summary

Always know if your food is high or low acid.

Use water bath canning only for high-acid foods.

Use pressure canning for low-acid foods.

Add acid when recommended to safely preserve borderline foods.

Follow tested, reliable recipes for safety.

Let's dive deeper into acidity and pH in canning with some more detailed info:

Deeper Dive: Acidity and pH in Canning

1. Clostridium botulinum's Role This bacterium produces botulinum toxin, one of the deadliest known toxins.

It thrives in low-acid, anaerobic (oxygen-free) environments — like canned low-acid foods sealed in jars.

Its spores cannot germinate unless the appropriate acidity is applied and heat is used. 2. Why pH 4.6?

pH 4.6 is the critical cutoff because Clostridium botulinum spores cannot grow below this acidity level.

Foods with pH ≤ 4.6 are considered safe for water bath canning since the acidity itself stops botulism growth.

3. How Acidity Affects Texture and Flavor

Adding acid (vinegar or lemon juice) not only ensures safety but can influence the final texture and taste.

For example, too much acid can make tomatoes too tart or pickles overly sour.

That's why tested recipes balance safety with flavor.

4. Testing and Measuring pH at Home

Although pH meters are available, they require calibration and proper use for accuracy.

pH test strips are less precise but can give a rough estimate.

Because of variability, most home canners rely on recommended acid amounts in trusted recipes.

5. Borderline Foods That Acidify Tomatoes vary widely in natural acidity depending on the variety and ripeness.

Recipes always call for acid to be added when canning tomatoes or products made from tomatoes. This includes: bottled lemon juice (two tablespoons) or half a teaspoon of citric acid per quart 1 tablespoon bottled lemon juice or 1/4 teaspoon of citric acid per pint

Using bottled lemon juice or citric acid is important because fresh lemons can vary in acidity.

6. Why Vinegar Acidity Matters

Vinegar's strength (acidity) varies from 4% to 7%, but the standard for canning is 5%.

Using a lower-acidity vinegar can make canned foods unsafe.

Always use vinegar labeled as 5% acidity for pickling and canning.

7. Acidity and Spoilage

A lack of acidity can result in spoilage, off-flavors, and the dangerous production of the botulism toxin. Even if jars seal properly, improperly acidified or processed foods can be unsafe.

8. High-Acid vs. Examples with Low-Acid Food Type Typical pH Range Canning Method

Apples 3.0 - 4.0 Water bath canning

Tomatoes 4.0-4.9* Depending on the recipe, add acid, a water bath, or pressure. Cucumbers (pickles) ~3.0 - 3.5 Water bath canning

Green beans 5.5 - 6.0 Pressure canning

Carrots 5.5 - 6.0 Pressure canning

Meat (chicken, beef) ~5.5 - 6.0 Pressure canning

*Tomatoes can be borderline, so acid addition is critical.

9. Steps for Safe Acidification & Canning

Use tested recipes from reliable sources (USDA, National Center for Home Food Preservation).

Just as directed, add a specific amount of acid (lemon juice, citric acid, or vinegar). Follow recommended processing times and methods (water bath or pressure).

Never alter acid levels or processing times without validated research.

Bonus: Common Mistakes to Avoid

making use of homemade vinegar without knowing how acidic it is. Assuming that all tomatoes are sufficiently acidic without acid. Using water bath canning for low-acid foods (meat, veggies).

Skipping pressure canning for low-acid foods, risking botulism.

Altering tested recipes by reducing acid or processing time.

Jar Types, Sizes, and Lid Systems

Here's a clear overview of jar types, sizes, and lid systems commonly used in home canning:

1. Jar sizes The Mason jar The classic canning jar is made of thick glass designed to withstand heat during processing. Available in regular or wide mouth.

Ball/Jar Brands

Standard mason jars and specialized jars for jams, jellies, pickles, and other items are available from common brands like Ball, Kerr, and Weck. Junk Jars German-style jars with glass lids and rubber gaskets, sealed with metal clips. Reusable lids but require careful sealing.

Kilner Jars

Similar to Weck, with glass lids and rubber seals, also clipped on. Often used for decorative or artisan canning.

2. Jar Sizes

Half a pint (250 milliliters) Perfect for jams, jellies, and small portions of preserves.

16 oz or 500 ml per pint The most popular size for canning fruits, sauces, and salsas.

Quart (32 oz / 1 liter)

Excellent for tomatoes, pickles, and larger batches. Half-gallon (64 oz / 2 liters)

Less common but used for large-batch canning or freezing.

3. Systems of Lids Two-Piece Lid System (Most Common)

Flat metal lid with a sealing compound: Single-use, creates a vacuum seal during processing.

Metal screw band (ring): Reusable, holds the lid in place during processing but removed after cooling.

Glass Lid with Rubber Gasket (Weck, Kilner)

A glass lid with a reusable rubber gasket forms the seal.

Metal clips or clamps hold the lid during processing.

The entire system is reusable but needs proper gasket care.

Plastic or Press-On Lids

Usually used for storage or refrigeration, but not for heat processing. Not recommended for water baths or pressure canning.

Quick Notes

Wide Mouth vs Regular Mouth: Wide mouth jars have a larger opening, easier to fill and removing contents, but lids and rings are not interchangeable with regular mouth jars.

Material: Always use jars specifically labeled for canning to withstand heat and pressure safely.

Lid Compatibility: Use new flat lids for each canning session (two-piece system). Rings can be reused if not damaged or rusted.

Here are some detailed tips on choosing jars and lids for different types of canning, plus how to sterilize and reuse them safely:

Choosing Jars & Lids for Different Canning Methods

1. Water Bath Canning

Used for high-acid foods (fruits, pickles, jams, jellies, tomatoes with added acid).

Jar type: Standard mason jars (Ball, Kerr, etc.) in pint or smaller sizes are ideal.

Lid system: Two-piece lids (flat metal lid + ring). Use new flat lids each time to ensure a proper vacuum seal. Rings can be reused.

Wide mouth jars are handy for chunky foods but regular mouth jars work fine for liquids.

2. Pressure Canning

Used for low-acid foods (vegetables, meats, soups, beans).

Type of jar: Standard mason jars in pint or quart sizes that can withstand high pressure and temperature. Lid system: The same two-piece lid system applies. Use new flat lids each time.

Use only jars labeled "canning" or "heat resistant" — avoid reuse of jars not intended for canning, such as store-bought pickle jars.

3. Specialty Jars

Due to differences in sealing, Weck and Kilner jars, which are beautiful and reusable, are less common in pressure canning. Better suited for refrigerator storage or water-bath canning. Reusing and sterilizing jars and lids Sterilizing Jars

If you plan to store canned goods for over a year or for very acidic foods, sterilize jars before filling them.

Methods:

Boiling Water Bath: Submerge jars in boiling water for 10 minutes.

Oven Method: Place jars in an oven at 225°F (107°C) for 20 minutes (do not preheat oven to avoid sudden heat shock).

Dishwasher: Hot cycle with no detergent can work for sterilizing jars if used immediately after.

Note: For many canning recipes, especially those involving a boiling water bath or pressure canner, sterilization before filling isn't necessary because the processing time sterilizes jars.

Reusable jars Inspect jars for cracks or chips before reuse—discard damaged jars.

Sterilize the jars if necessary by washing them in hot, soapy water or the dishwasher. Store clean jars with lids off to avoid odors or dust.

Reusing Lids

Flat lids (two-piece system): Should NOT be reused for canning because the sealing compound wears out after one use.

Rings: Can be reused indefinitely if not rusty or bent.

Weck/Kilner rubber gaskets: Reusable but replace if brittle, cracked, or no longer flexible.

Additional Tips

Rings should only be tightened until they are "finger-tight" to allow air to escape during canning, so don't tighten them too much before processing. Check the seal after it has cooled, then take the rings out for storage. Store sealed jars in a cool, dark place to preserve quality and safety.

Label jars with date and contents for easy tracking.

Chapter 2: Preparing for Success

Sterilizing Jars and Equipment

Sterilizing jars and equipment is a crucial step in canning to prevent spoilage and ensure food safety. Here's a detailed guide on how to properly sterilize jars and equipment:

When Jars Need to Be Sterilized If the processing time is less than ten minutes, jars must be sterilized, regardless of whether you use a pressure canner or a water bath. If the recipe requires 10 minutes or more of processing, sterilization of jars is not strictly necessary, as they will be sterilized during canning.

Jar Sterilization Methods 1. Boiling Water Method (Most Common)

Wash jars in hot, soapy water. Rinse thoroughly.

Place jars upright in a large pot or water bath canner.

Water should cover the entire thing, at least an inch above the jars. Boil the water for ten minutes after it comes to a boil, adding one minute for every 1,000 feet above sea level. Keep jars in hot water until ready to fill.

2. Oven Method (Not Recommended by USDA)

While still used by some, this method is not recommended by food safety experts due to the risk of glass breakage and uneven heating.

3. Dishwasher (With Sanitizing Cycle)

Only if the sanitizer cycle in your dishwasher has high temperatures (over 170°F/77°C). Run through the sanitize cycle and keep jars hot until use.

Sterilizing Lids and Bands

Lids (flats) should not be boiled. Instead, heat them in simmering water (180°F/82°C) for a few minutes to soften the sealing compound.

Bands (rings) do not need to be sterilized; however, they should be washed thoroughly in hot, soapy water. Other Equipment

Use boiling water or a diluted bleach solution (1 tbsp unscented liquid bleach per gallon of water) to sanitize canning tools like:

Jar lifters

Funnels

Bubble removers

Ladles

Rinse with clean water after using bleach.

Tips for Safe Canning

Only use mason-style canning jars made for preserving.

Don't reuse commercial jars (e.g., from store-bought pasta sauce).

Always inspect jars for chips or cracks before use.

Preparing Your Workspace

It is essential to prepare your workspace for canning for safety, efficiency, and food quality. Here's a step-by-step guide to help you set up your canning area properly:

1. Clean and Sanitize Your Workspace

Clear the counters: To create a space that is open and free of clutter, get rid of anything that isn't necessary. Wipe down surfaces: Use hot, soapy water to clean countertops, sinks, and tables. Sanitize with a food-safe solution (1 tablespoon bleach to 1-gallon water if needed).

Wash your hands thoroughly before handling food or equipment.

2. Collect all of the Tools Make sure you have all tools clean and within reach:

Water bath canner or pressure canner (depending on the recipe)

Canning jars (check for cracks or chips)

New lids and clean bands

Jar lifter

Bubble remover/headspace tool

Funnel

Ladle

Clean towels and dishcloths

Cooling rack or a thick towel for finished jars

3. Prepare the lids and jars. Rinse thoroughly jars, lids, and bands in hot, soapy water. If your processing time is less than ten minutes, sterilize the jars: Boil in water for 10 minutes or run through a hot dishwasher cycle.

Keep jars warm until use (in hot water or a warm oven).

If you're using traditional metal lids, warm them in hot (but not boiling) water to soften the sealing compound. 4. Organize Ingredients and Recipes

Prepare all meats, vegetables, and fruits by washing them. Use a tested and reliable canning recipe (from USDA, Ball®, etc.).

Make sure to measure the ingredients and have spices, salt, and vinegar on hand in case they are needed. 5. Set Up Your Canning Station

Divide your space into zones:

The cutting board, knife, and mixing bowls are in the prep zone. Filling Zone: Hot jars, funnel, ladle, ingredients.

Processing Zone: Canner on the stove and a jar lifter nearby Cooling Zone: Towels or rack to set hot jars for 12–24 hours undisturbed.

6. Check Safety Measures

Ensure adequate lighting and ventilation. If you're using a pressure canner, double-check that the dial, vent, and gasket are working properly. Avoid distractions because canning necessitates total focus for safety and timing reasons.

Choosing the Right Recipes

It is essential to concentrate on safety, shelf stability, and compatibility with the canning method when selecting canning recipes. Here's a guide to help you select the best recipes:

1. Choose Tested and Approved Recipes

Always use recipes that come from trustworthy sources like: The Whole USDA Guide to Home Canning National Center for Home Food Preservation (NCHFP)

Canning books from Ball® and Kerr® University extension services (like Penn State or Michigan State)

The processing times and safe acidity levels of these recipes have been tested in a laboratory. 2. Match the Right Canning Method to the Recipe Water Bath Canning (for high-acid foods)

Use only on foods with a pH of 4.6 or lower. Common examples:

Jellies and jams Pickles

Tomatoes (with added acid)

Butter made from fruits Salsas (only recipes that have been tried and approved) Pressure Canning (for low-acid foods)

Required for anything with a pH higher than 4.6, such as:

Corn, beans, and carrots are vegetables. Meats and poultry

Seafood

stews and soups (when safe guidelines are followed) Chili and other mixed-ingredient meals

3. Avoid recipes that aren't approved or safe. Dairy products, such as soups made with butter or cream, cannot be canned. No canning of flour or starch-thickened sauces (unless the recipe specifies a safe method)

No "creative" or untested canning of low-acid foods in a water bath

Be cautious with online recipes—always verify them against a trusted source

4. Take into Account Preferences and Availability of Ingredients Choose recipes that:

Make use of abundant or in-season produce. Fit your family's eating habits

Store well and are useful year-round (e.g., pasta sauces, relishes, soups)

5. Start Simple if You're New to Canning

Good beginner recipes:

Strawberry jam

Dill pickles

Applesauce

Crushed tomatoes (with lemon juice or citric acid)

Understanding Headspace, Processing Times, and Altitude Adjustments

Understanding headspace, processing times, and altitude adjustments is crucial for safe and effective home canning. Each concept is broken down as follows: 1. Headspace

Definition:

The space that exists between the underside of the lid and the surface of the food or liquid in the jar is called the headspace. Why It Matters:

Allows for food expansion during processing.

Ensures a proper vacuum seal.

Too little headspace can lead to food being forced out of the jar.

There is a risk of spoilage or improper sealing due to excessive headspace. Standard Headspace Guidelines:

Jams/Jellies: ¼ inch

12 inches for fruits and tomatoes (acid foods). Low-acid foods (vegetables, meats, soups): 1 inch

2. Processing Times

Definition:

This is the time jars must be heated during canning to destroy harmful microorganisms and enzymes that cause spoilage.

Determined By:

Type of food (low-acid vs. high-acid)

Size of the jar Food density (chunky vs. pureed)

Method of packing (hot pack versus raw pack) Key Points:

In a boiling water bath, high-acid foods like tomatoes, fruits, and pickles can be safely processed. Low-acid foods (vegetables, meats, legumes) must be processed in a pressure canner to reach 240°F, necessary to kill Clostridium botulinum spores.

Always follow tested recipes from trusted sources like:

USDA Complete Guide to Home Canning

Ball/Bernardin canning books

Services for university extension 3. Altitude Adjustments

Why It Matters:

At higher altitudes, water boils at lower temperatures, necessitating an increase in processing times or pressures to ensure safety. Adjustments:

For Boiling Water Bath Canning:

Increase processing time as altitude increases:

Altitude (ft) Add to Time

1,001–3,000 Add 5 minutes

3,001–6,000 Add 10 minutes

6,001–8,000 Add 15 minutes

8,001–10,000 Add 20 minutes

For Pressure Canning:

Increase pressure as altitude increases.

Dial-Gauge Pressure Canner:

Pressure (PSI) Altitude in feet 0–2,000 11 PSI

2,001–4,000 12 PSI

4,001–6,000 13 PSI

6,001–8,000 14 PSI

Weighted-Gauge Pressure Canner:

Use 10 PSI below 1,000 ft.

Use 15 PSI above 1,000 ft.

Chapter 3: Water Bath Canning

High-Acid Foods Explained

In canning, high-acid foods are foods that have a pH of 4.6 or lower. Clostridium botulinum, the bacterium that causes botulism, a potentially fatal form of food poisoning, cannot grow at this level of acidity. Because of their acidity, high-acid foods can be safely canned using a boiling water bath canner, rather than a pressure canner.

Common High-Acid Foods:

Most fruits (e.g., apples, peaches, berries, cherries, plums, citrus fruits)

To ensure their safety, tomatoes frequently require an additional acid like citric or lemon juice. Juices of fruits Pickled foods (vinegar significantly increases acidity)

preserves, jellies, and jams made from acidic fruits Key Points for Safe Canning of High-Acid Foods:

Use a water bath canner: Boiling water (212°F/100°C) is hot enough to kill mold, yeast, and most bacteria in high-acid foods.

Add acid when needed: Tomatoes and some borderline fruits may need added lemon juice, vinegar, or citric acid.

Use guidelines from reliable sources like the USDA or university extension programs to ensure safe pH levels and processing times. Follow tried-and-true recipes. Seal and store properly: Jars must seal correctly and be stored in a cool, dark place to prevent spoilage.

Here's a deeper look into high-acid foods in canning, including why pH matters, borderline foods, acidification, and safety tips:

Why pH Matters in Canning

The pH scale measures how acidic or basic a substance is. It ranges from 0 (extremely acidic) to 14 (extremely basic), with 7 representing neutrality. Clostridium botulinum spores can survive in low-acid environments (pH above 4.6) and grow in the absence of oxygen—like inside a sealed jar.

At pH 4.6 or lower, these spores cannot grow or produce the botulinum toxin, making canning with boiling water (which doesn't reach pressure canning temps) safe.

Examples of High-Acid Foods (pH ≤ 4.6)

Fruits:

Apples (pH ~3.3–4.0)

Berries (strawberries, raspberries, blueberries)

Cherries

Citrus fruits (oranges, lemons, limes, grapefruits)

Peaches

Pears

Pineapples

Plums

Fruit Products:

Applesauce

Juices of fruits Fruit preserves, jams, jellies

Pickled Items:

Vinegar-based pickled vegetables Vinegar-based chutneys and relishes Only when vinegar is properly added can vegetables like beets, cucumbers, peppers, and onions be picked. Borderline-Acid Foods (Must Be Acidified)

Some foods are close to the 4.6 pH threshold and must be acidified before boiling water canning:

Tomatoes (pH 4.2–4.9)

Must be acidified with bottled lemon juice (1 tbsp/quart), vinegar, or citric acid (¼ tsp/quart).

Depending on the variety and degree of ripeness, figs, pears, and melon may also require acidification. Acidification Tips:

Lemon juice: Use bottled lemon juice for consistent acidity (fresh lemons vary in pH).

Citric acid: This acid comes in a powdered form and is very effective. One teaspoon per gallon is common. Vinegar: Should be 5% acidity—do not dilute unless the recipe says so.

Why Use Water Bath Canning for Foods with a Lot of Acid? For yeast, molds, and the majority of bacteria, spoilage organisms can be eradicated by boiling water to 212°F/100°C. When the acid levels are right, safe preservation can be achieved without the use of pressure. This is a popular home canning method because it requires less equipment and takes less time to process. Safety Best Practices

Use up-to-date, tested recipes (USDA, National Center for Home Food Preservation, Ball, university extensions).

Don't alter acid, sugar, or vinegar levels in recipes—these are crucial for safety.

Always make sure the jars are sealed correctly and store them in a cool, dry, dark place. Jars should be labeled with the date and contents; use them within one to two years.

Step-by-Step Water Bath Canning Process

For preserving high-acid foods like fruits, jams, pickles, salsas, and tomatoes (with added acid), this clear step-by-step guide to the water bath canning process is ideal: Tools You'll Need:

Canner with a water bath (or a deep pot with a rack and lid) Canning jars (mason jars)

New lids and clean screw bands

Jar raiser Funnel

Bubble remover or non-metallic spatula

Clean cloth or paper towel

A cooling rack or towel Step-by-Step Water Bath Canning:

1. Get the lids and jars ready. Wash jars, lids, and bands in hot soapy water. Rinse well.

Keep jars hot until ready to fill (in hot water, dishwasher, or oven set to low). This prevents thermal shock.

Heat lids (if recommended by the manufacturer) in a small pan of hot—not boiling—water.

2. Prepare the Recipe

Cook your high-acid food (e.g., jam, salsa, fruit preserve) according to a tested canning recipe.

Keep it hot and ready for filling.

3. Fill the Jars

Place a funnel in the hot jar.

Ladle the hot food into jars, leaving the appropriate headspace (usually ¼" for jams/jellies, ½" for fruits/pickles).

Remove air bubbles by sliding a bubble remover or spatula along the inside edge of the jar.

Wipe the rim with a clean, damp cloth to remove any food residue.

4. Apply the Lids and Bands

Center the lid on the jar.

Apply the screw band and tighten it to the fingertip tight (snug but not overly tight).

5. Place Jars in the Canner

Use a jar lifter to place jars upright on the rack in the water bath canner.

Ensure jars are covered by at least 1–2 inches of water.

6. Heat and Process

Cover the canner with a lid and bring water to a full rolling boil.

Start timing once boiling begins.

Process for the time specified in your tested recipe (based on food type, jar size, and altitude).

7. Put the heat off and relax. Once the processing time is up, turn off the heat.

Let the jars sit in the canner for 5 minutes with the lid off.

8. Remove Jars and Cool

Lift jars out using the jar lifter and place them upright on a towel or cooling rack.

Jars should not be tilted or wiped. Let them cool undisturbed for 12–24 hours.

9. Check Seals

After 12–24 hours, check the lids for a proper seal (the center should be concave and not flex when pressed).

Remove the screw bands and wipe the jars clean.

Date and the contents of the label 10. Store Properly

Store sealed jars in a cool, dark, and dry place.

For the best quality, use within one year. Use any unsealed jars within a few days by storing them in the refrigerator. If you want, I can provide a printable checklist version or help you convert this into a guide tailored to a specific recipe (like jam or pickles).

Troubleshooting Water Bath Issues

Here's a troubleshooting guide for common water bath canning issues, broken down by symptoms with causes and solutions:

1. Jars aren't covered in water. Cause: Too little water was added at the beginning, or the level was reduced by boiling. Fix: Add boiling water to ensure jars are covered by at least 1–2 inches. Never add cold water during processing.

2. Jars Overturning Cause: Improper jar placement or rapid boiling.

Fix: Use a rack to keep jars stable, and ensure a gentle, rolling boil, not a rapid one.

3. During the processing, water stops boiling. Cause: Too much lid removal or too little heat. Fix: Maintain a steady rolling boil for the entire processing time. Start timing only once boiling resumes after jars are added.

4. Jars Break in the Canner

Cause: Sudden temperature changes or using cracked/old jars.

Fix:

Pre-warm jars and food.

Avoid placing cold jars into boiling water.

Inspect jars for chips and cracks before use.

5. Jars Don't Seal

Cause: Inadequate processing, faulty lids, or improper headspace.

Fix:

Reprocess within 24 hours with new lids.

Ensure correct headspace and clean jar rims before sealing.

Check for consistent boiling and correct time.

6. Water is Cloudy After Processing

Cause: Hard water or starch/sugar residue.

Fix:

Add 1–2 tablespoons of white vinegar to the water.

Rinse or wipe jars after removing them from the canner.

7. Siphoning (Liquid Loss in Jars)

Cause: Rapid temperature changes or over-tightening lids.

Fix:

Use gentle boiling.

After turning off the heat, allow the jars to rest for five minutes in the canner. Tighten bands finger-tight, not too tight.

8. Food in Jars Floats Cause: Loose packing or underprocessing.

Fix:

Food should be packed tightly but not too tightly. Make use of appropriate headspace and processing time. 9. Rings or Lids with Rust Cause: Leaving jars wet or improper storage.

Fix:

Before storing, thoroughly dry it out. Without the rings on, store in a cool, dry location. Here are additional troubleshooting tips for water bath canning issues that go beyond the basics, including safety concerns and post-processing problems:

10. Jars Seal, Then Unseal Later

Cause: Weak vacuum due to improper headspace, debris on rims, or processing errors.

Fix:

Always use a damp, clean cloth to clean the rims. Reprocess within 24 hours if unsealed (using a new lid).

Ensure correct processing time and headspace.

11. Food Spoilage Despite Proper Seal

Cause: Underprocessing, poor quality ingredients, or storage issues.

Fix:

Always follow tested recipes (like from Ball, NCHFP, or university extensions).

Discard jars with off smells, bubbling, or discoloration.

Store sealed jars in a cool, dark place (50–70°F).

12. Jar Contents Boil Over During Processing

Cause: Too little headspace or overfilled jars.

Fix:

Follow recipe instructions for correct headspace (usually ¼" to ½").

Overtightening lids can lead to pressure buildup.

13. Excessive Air Bubbles in Jar After Processing

Cause: Not removing air pockets or too rapid heating.

Fix:

Use a non-metallic utensil to remove air bubbles before sealing.

Gently tap jar sides if needed.

Be sure food is packed firmly but not crushed.

14. Food that is cloudy, darkened, or discolored Causes:

Darkening: Too much processing, too much light, or too much air. Fading: Overcooking or light exposure. Cloudiness: Starch, minerals, or spoilage.

Fix:

Use fresh, quality produce.

Add vinegar or lemon juice if called for.

Store in a dark place; avoid excessive boiling.

15. Sticky Jars After Processing

Cause: Siphoning or seepage during processing.

Fix:

Wipe jars with a clean, damp cloth after cooling.

Recheck seals.

Prevent future issues by avoiding rapid temperature changes.

16. Rings Won't Come Off Easily

Cause: Sticking is caused by syrup or juice residue.
Fix:

Soak in warm, soapy water and gently twist.

Don't store jars with rings on — store without bands to prevent rust and false seals.

Chapter 4: Pressure Canning

Low-Acid Foods and the Need for Pressure

Low-acid foods must be pressure canned because of the risk of botulism, a deadly form of food poisoning caused by the bacteria Clostridium botulinum. Here's a clear explanation of why:

What Are Low-Acid Foods?

Foods with low acidity do not naturally prevent the growth of bacteria because their pH is higher than 4.6. Common examples include:

Vegetables (green beans, corn, carrots, potatoes)

Meats (fish, beef, and poultry) Poultry and game

Soups and stews

Some legumes (beans, lentils)

Reasons Why Pressure Canning Is Required Clostridium botulinum spores can survive boiling water (212°F / 100°C).

The only way to kill these spores at temperatures above 240°F (116°C) is to use a pressure canner. Botulism spores in low-acid foods cannot be eradicated by water bath canning. How Pressure Canning Works

A pressure canner is used to sterilize sealed jars. Steam builds up under pressure, raising the temperature.

Processing times are based on the type of food, jar size, and altitude to ensure all spores are destroyed.

Safe Canning Principles for Low-Acid Foods

Always use a pressure canner (not a pressure cooker).

Follow tested recipes from trusted sources (like USDA, Ball, or Extension services).

Adjust for altitude—higher elevations require longer processing or more pressure.

Do not attempt to shortcut processing times or cooling procedures.

Here's a more detailed breakdown of why low-acid foods require pressure canning, how it works, and the science and safety behind it:

Low-Acid Foods and the Need for Pressure Canning (Extended Guide)

Understanding Food Acidity

High-acid foods: pH 4.6 or lower

Tomatoes (some varieties), fruits, pickled vegetables (acidified with vinegar or lemon juice)

Safely canned using a water bath canner

Low-acid foods: pH above 4.6

Most vegetables, meats, poultry, seafood, and dairy

Require pressure canning to be shelf-stable and safe

The Danger: Clostridium botulinum

Botulism is caused by a toxin produced by Clostridium botulinum.

These spores are:

Ubiquitous in soil and water

Not destroyed by boiling water

Thrive in anaerobic (oxygen-free) environments, like sealed jars

Can germinate in low-acid conditions and produce a deadly neurotoxin

Why Water Bath Canning Isn't Enough

Boiling water reaches only 212°F (100°C) at sea level.

Some microbes can be destroyed at this temperature, but botulism spores cannot. Low-acid foods in a boiling water bath may look and smell fine but can be toxic and deadly.

How Pressure Canning Prevents Botulism

Pressure canners trap steam, increasing internal temperature to 240–250°F (116–121°C).

This destroys botulism spores reliably when held for a safe processing time.

The time and pressure required depends on:

Type of food

Size of jar

Altitude (longer times or higher pressure are required at higher altitudes) Examples of Low-Acid Foods That Must Be Pressure Canned

Food Type Examples

Vegetables Green beans, carrots, peas, corn, beets

Meats Chicken, beef, pork, game meat

Soups/Stews Vegetable soup, chili, beef stew

Lentils, including pinto beans and black beans
Seafood Fish, shellfish

Broths/Stocks Bone broth, chicken stock

Best Practices for Pressure Canning

Use only tested, approved recipes

From sources like the USDA, National Center for Home Food Preservation, or Ball

Always use a pressure canner, not a regular pressure cooker

Maintain correct pressure throughout the processing

Use a weighted gauge or dial gauge (check for calibration annually)

Adjust for altitude

Pressure must be increased for higher elevations

Cool naturally

Never force-cool the canner. Let the pressure drop naturally before opening.

Safety Tips for Pressure Canning Before using, inspect jars and lids. Follow exact preparation steps (peeling, packing, liquid levels)

Keep a canning log or batch record

Store in a cool, dark place

If in doubt about a sealed jar—throw it out

Types of Pressure Canners

1. Weighted Gauge Pressure Canner

How it works: Uses a weight to regulate pressure. The weight rocks or jiggles to indicate that the correct pressure is being maintained.

Pressure settings: Typically has fixed pressure settings—5, 10, and 15 pounds (psi).

Adjustment for altitude: You adjust pressure by changing the weight used.

Pros:

No need to monitor a dial gauge constantly.

Less prone to calibration issues.

Cons:

Due to the weight's rocking and jiggling, it can be noisy. Less precise for certain recipes compared to a dial gauge.

2. Dial Gauge Pressure Canner

How it works: Has a dial that shows the exact pressure inside the canner.

Pressure settings: Can be set to and monitored at any pressure level, allowing for more precise control.

Adjustment for altitude: Adjust the pressure setting based on your altitude.

Pros:

Allows for precise monitoring of pressure. Quiet operation.

Cons:

Requires yearly calibration of the dial for accuracy (through extension offices or the manufacturer).

You must watch the dial during the entire process.

Electric Pressure Canners are a type of bonus How it works: Uses built-in electronics to regulate temperature and pressure.

Examples: Presto Electric Digital Pressure Canner.

Pros:

Automated and user-friendly.

Great for small batches.

Cons:

Not all are USDA-approved for low-acid foods.

Less flexible and may not accommodate large jars or multiple batches.

Step-by-Step Pressure Canning Process

The following is a step-by-step, printable guide for the pressure canning process: Step-by-Step Pressure Canning Process

Prepare the Materials and Equipment Canning jars, lids, and bands should be cleaned and sterilized. Prepare your food according to your recipe.

Empty Jars Pack food into jars, leaving the recommended headspace (usually 1/4 to 1 inch depending on the recipe).

Remove air bubbles with a non-metallic spatula or bubble remover.

Wipe jar rims clean with a damp cloth to ensure a good seal.

Use Bands and Lids. Screw bands onto jar lids until they are snug but not too tight with a fingertip. Fill the Pressure Canner with water. The pressure canner should be filled with the recommended amount of hot water, usually 2 to 3 inches. Load Jars into Canner

Place jars on the rack inside the canner, ensuring they do not touch each other or the sides.

Close and Seal the Canner

Secure the lid on the pressure canner according to manufacturer instructions.

Vent the Canner

Leave the weight or petcock open and heat until steam flows steadily for 10 minutes to remove air.

Pressurize the Canner

Close the vent (place the weight or close the petcock).

Allow pressure to rise to the number of pounds per square inch (PSI) that is appropriate for your altitude (typically 10, 11, or 15 PSI). Start Timing

Once the correct pressure is reached, start timing according to the recipe's processing time.

Maintain Pressure

Adjust heat to maintain steady pressure throughout the processing time.

Do not let pressure drop or rise above the recommended level.

Cool Down

When processing time ends, turn off the heat and let the canner cool naturally until the pressure drops to zero (do NOT force cool).

Open the canning jar. To avoid steam burns, unlock and remove the lid as soon as the pressure is completely released. Remove and Cool Jars

Carefully remove jars with a jar lifter and place them on a towel or cooling rack.

Let jars cool undisturbed for 12–24 hours.

Check Seals and Label

After the jars cool, check the seals by pressing the center of the lids.

Label jars with contents and date.

Proper storage Store jars in a cool, dark, dry place.

Here's a more detailed, expanded version of the Pressure Canning Process including tips, troubleshooting, and altitude adjustments:

Detailed Step-by-Step Pressure Canning Process

1. Prepare Equipment and Ingredients

Inspect jars for cracks or chips. Mason jars are the only canning jars that should be used. Rinse thoroughly jars, lids, and bands in hot, soapy water. Keep jars warm until use to prevent breakage when hot food is added (place in simmering water or dishwasher on warm).

Use new lids each time for a proper seal.

Follow established, tried-and-true recipe guidelines when preparing food. 2. Fill Jars

Pack hot food into jars, following recipe headspace instructions (usually 1/4" for fruits, 1" for low-acid foods).

Remove trapped air bubbles by running a non-metallic spatula or bubble remover along the inside edge of the jar.

Wipe jar rims carefully with a clean damp cloth to remove food residue or liquid for a good seal.

3. Apply Lids and Bands

Place the flat lid on the rim of the jar. Screw the metal band down just until the fingertip is tight; do not overtighten, as air must escape during processing.

4. Add Water to the Pressure Canner

Following the manufacturer's instructions, fill the pressure canner's bottom with 2 to 3 inches of hot water. The water creates steam to build pressure.

5. Load Jars into the Canner

Place the rack at the bottom of the canner (to prevent jars from touching the base).

Place the jars on the rack so that they don't touch the canner walls or each other. Leave space between jars for even heat circulation.

6. Close and Seal the Canner

Securely close the lid according to your pressure canner model's instructions.

7. Vent the Canner (Exhaust Air)

Leave the petcock or vent pipe open and turn the heat up to high. Allow steam to vent steadily for 10 minutes—this drives air out of the canner to ensure proper pressure and temperature.

8. Pressurize the Canner

Place the weight or close the petcock to seal the canner.

Pressure will begin to rise.

9. Adjust Heat and Start Timing

When the correct pressure (PSI) is reached:

For dial gauge canners: the pressure indicator reaches the desired number.

For weighted gauge canners: weight starts to jiggle or rock.

Lower heat to maintain steady pressure and start timing based on the recipe (usually 20–90 minutes depending on food type and jar size).

10. Monitor Pressure

Adjust the heat to maintain a constant pressure without fluctuations and check the pressure on a regular basis. Do NOT remove the weight or open the petcock during processing.

11. End Processing Time and Cool Down

When the processing time ends, turn off the heat.

Let the canner depressurize naturally—do NOT open the lid or force cool (this can cause jar breakage or food spoilage).

Pressure will drop to zero; the pressure indicator will show this.

12. Open the Canner Safely

Unlock and remove the lid, lifting it away from your face to avoid steam burns.

13. Remove Jars and Cool

Use a jar lifter to carefully remove jars.

Place jars upright on a towel or rack, leaving space for air to circulate.

Do not disturb jars for 12–24 hours to allow sealing.

14. Check Seals

After cooling, press the center of each lid: it should be concave and not flex or pop.

Test the sealed lids by lightly lifting them after removing the screw bands; they will withstand pressure. Refrigerate any unsealed jars and consume them promptly.

15. Label and Store

Label jars with contents and date.

The ideal temperature range for storage is between 50 and 70 degrees Fahrenheit, or 10 and 21 degrees Celsius. Avoid freezing or direct sunlight.

Additional Tips and Information

Changes to the altitude: Increase pressure as altitude rises because water boils at lower temperatures.

For example:

Sea level to 1,000 ft: 10 PSI

1,001 to 3,000 ft: 11 PSI

3,001 to 6,000 ft: 12 PSI or 15 PSI depending on your canner

Check your local extension service for exact altitude recommendations.

Use Only Tested Recipes:

To ensure safety, adhere to USDA-tested recipes or those from reliable sources. Troubleshooting:

Jar breakage: Avoid sudden temperature changes; warm jars before filling.

Seals fail: Check rim cleanliness; don't overtighten lids; use new lids.

Pressure doesn't build: Check the canner lid seal and vent pipe for blockage.

Maintenance:

Regularly check your pressure gauge accuracy yearly and replace it if needed.

Safety Tips and Common Mistakes

For your convenience, we've compiled a concise list of Pressure Canning Safety Tips and Common

Errors: Tips for Pressure Canning Safety Use a Tested Recipe: Always follow USDA-approved or trusted canning recipes to ensure safe acidity and processing times.

Check Your Equipment: Inspect your pressure canner's gasket, vent pipe, and safety valves before each use to ensure they're clean and functioning.

Follow Venting Instructions: Vent your canner for 10 minutes before pressurizing to remove air and allow steam to fill the canner properly.

Maintain the Correct Pressure: To kill harmful bacteria like Clostridium botulinum, use the pressure in the recipe, adjusting for your altitude if necessary. Avoid Overfilling Jars: Leave proper headspace (usually 1 inch) to allow for expansion and proper vacuum seal.

Use the Right Jars and Lids: Use canning-specific jars and lids; do not reuse single-use lids.

Do Not Force-Open: Let the canner cool naturally and release pressure before opening. Opening too soon can cause burns and spoil jars.

Cool Jars Properly: Let jars cool undisturbed for 12–24 hours before checking seals to avoid seal failures.

Label and Store Safely: Label jars with date and contents. Store in a cool, dark, dry place.

Common Pressure Canning Errors Skipping Venting: Not venting the canner properly can trap air, leading to inaccurate pressure and unsafe food.

Using Incorrect Pressure: Using too low pressure can fail to kill bacteria; too high pressure can damage jars or equipment.

Overfilling Jars: Overfilled jars can overflow, preventing proper sealing and causing spoilage.

Utilizing Old or Damaged Equipment: Unsafe pressure levels can be caused by rusted canners, clogged vents, and worn gaskets. Not Adjusting for Altitude: Higher altitudes require higher pressures; failing to adjust can result in underprocessing.

Ignoring Headspace Guidelines: Incorrect headspace leads to seal failure or jar breakage.

Reusing Lids: Single-use lids should not be reused as they may not seal properly.

Removing Jars Too Early: Handling or cooling jars improperly can break seals or contaminate contents.

Using Non-Canning Jars: Under pressure canning, regular glass jars, such as those from store-bought food, may break. Failing to Clean Jar Rims: Food residue on jar rims can prevent lids from sealing correctly.

For pressure canning, the following are more in-depth Safety Tips and Common Errors, delving deeper into both pitfalls and best practices: Tips for Pressure Canning Safety Extras Use a Reliable Pressure Gauge: If your canner has a dial gauge, test it annually for accuracy at your local extension office or a trusted service.

Keep the Vent Pipe Clear: After each use, make sure the vent pipe is free from debris to allow steam to escape properly.

Use Canning-Specific Salt: If your recipe calls for salt, use canning or pickling salt, which doesn't contain additives that can cloud or affect safety.

Avoid Using Old Recipes: Recipes over 20 years old may not meet current safety standards; always update your methods.

Don't Rush the Process: Allow the canner to reach and maintain full pressure for the entire recommended time to ensure safety.

Caution is advised with low-acid foods because meats, vegetables, and soups can support Clostridium botulinum growth and must be pressure-canned. Wear Protective Gloves: Handling hot jars and equipment can cause burns; always use oven mitts or jar lifters.

Keep Children and Pets Away: Pressure canners get very hot and heavy; keep your canning area clear.

Inspect Jars Before Use: Discard any jars with chips or cracks to prevent breakage under pressure.

Store Processed Jars Away from Heat and Light: Prolonged heat or sunlight can degrade food quality and seal integrity.

More Common Mistakes to Avoid

Not following the recipe exactly: Canned food can be unsafe if the ingredients are changed, especially the acidity or processing time. Using Non-Standard Jars or Lids: Mason jars and lids are designed to handle canning conditions; substitutes may fail.

Overloading the Canner: Crowding jars can interfere with steam circulation and proper heat distribution.

Not Monitoring Pressure During Processing: Pressure can drop unexpectedly; monitor gauges or weighted lids closely.

Using Dirty or Damaged Lids: Even a tiny dent or rust can cause seal failure.

Tightening Lids Too Much Before Processing: Lids should be "finger-tight," not overly tightened, to allow air to escape during processing.

Not Allowing Pressure to Return to Zero Naturally: Forcing open the vent or lid while pressure remains can cause injury and spoilage.

Ignoring Signs of Spoilage After Canning: Swollen lids, leaks, foul odors, or mold are signs the food is unsafe to eat.

Reusing Sealed Jars: Once a jar seal is broken, the jar should be washed and inspected before reuse, but never reuse the lid.

Failing to Label Jars: Without dates, you risk consuming food past the recommended shelf life (usually up to 1 year).

Chapter 5: Canning Recipes – Fruits & Jams

Whole and Sliced Fruits in Syrup

Using the water bath canning method, here is a clear, step-by-step guide for canning whole and sliced fruits in syrup: Canning Whole and Sliced Fruits in Syrup
 Ingredients:
 Fresh, ripe fruit (whole or sliced)
 Water
 Sugar (to make syrup)
 Lemon juice or ascorbic acid (optional, to prevent browning)
 Equipment:
 Banded and lidded canning jars Large water bath pot or canner Jar lifter and funnel
 Ladle
 Clean cloth or paper towels
 Timer
 Step 1: Prepare the Syrup
 Make your syrup by dissolving sugar in water. Common kinds of syrup: Light syrup: 2 cups sugar + 4 cups water
 Medium syrup: 3 cups sugar + 4 cups water
 4 cups sugar and 4 cups water make a thick syrup. Heat until sugar dissolves; keep syrup hot.

Step 2: Prepare the Fruit

Wash fruit thoroughly.

Peel, core, pit, or slice as needed.

To prevent browning (especially for apples, pears, peaches), soak fruit in water with lemon juice or ascorbic acid solution for 5 minutes.

Step 3: Pack the Jars

Pack the prepared fruit into hot sterilized jars:

Whole fruit: pack gently to avoid bruising.

Sliced fruit: pack carefully to avoid air pockets.

Pour hot syrup over the fruit, leaving ½ inch headspace.

Step 4: Remove Air Bubbles

Use a non-metallic spatula or bubble remover tool to slide along jar sides to release trapped air.

Adjust headspace if necessary by adding more syrup.

Step 5: Clean Jar Rims and Seal

Wipe jar rims clean with a damp cloth.

Place sterilized lids on jars.

Screw on bands fingertip-tight (not too tight).

Step 6: Process in Water Bath

Place jars on a rack in the canner.

Make sure that water covers the jars by at least 1-2 inches. Bring water to a full boil and process according to fruit type and jar size:

Fruit Type	Jar Size	Processing Time (minutes)
Apples (whole/sliced)	Pint or Quart	20 minutes
Peaches	Pint or Quart	20 minutes
Pears	Pint or Quart	20 minutes

Cherries (pitted) 25 minutes per pint or gallon Adjust times for altitude (add 1 minute for every 1000 ft above 1000 ft elevation).

Step 7: Cool and Store

Remove jars with jar lifter and place on towel or cooling rack.

Let cool undisturbed for 12-24 hours.

Check seals (lid should not flex up/down when pressed).

Label jars with date and contents.

Store in a cool, dark place.

For canning whole and sliced fruits in syrup, a more in-depth and expanded guide with additional advice, syrup options, handling delicate fruits, and troubleshooting procedures is provided here.

Detailed Guide: Canning Whole and Sliced Fruits in Syrup

1. Choosing and Preparing Fruit

Select: Use fresh, ripe, and blemish-free fruit. Overripe or bruised fruit will not preserve well.

Wash: Rinse under cool running water.

Peel (if needed): For fruits like peaches, apricots, or pears, blanch in boiling water for 30-60 seconds, then cool in ice water to loosen skins.

Slice or pit: Slice into uniform sizes so that processing and packing are uniform. Pit peaches or cherries. Prevent Browning: For fruits like apples, pears, peaches:

Soak slices in water + 1 tablespoon lemon juice per quart of water for 5-10 minutes.

Alternatively, use ascorbic acid powder or commercial anti-darkening products.

2. Syrup Preparation

Types of Syrup (sugar + water):

Syrup Type	Sugar	Water	Use For
Light	2 cups	4 cups	Delicate fruits, low sugar preference
Medium	3 cups	4 cups	Most fruits (balanced sweetness)
Heavy	4 cups	4 cups	Very sweet fruit or preferred sweetness

For fruit canned without sugar (in plain water or juice), adjust processing times accordingly.

3. Packing Jars

Use hot jars to prevent cracking when adding hot syrup.

Fill jars with fruit, leaving ½ inch headspace.

Pour hot syrup over fruit to cover, maintaining headspace.

Remove air bubbles by sliding a non-metallic spatula around the inside of the jar.

If necessary, adjust the level of syrup.

4. Sealing

Wipe jar rims with a clean damp cloth to remove syrup or fruit residue.

Place sterilized lids on jars and screw bands fingertip-tight.

Avoid overtightening, which can prevent proper sealing.

5. Processing in Water Bath

Place jars on a rack in a canner or large pot.

Fill the jars to the top by 1 to 2 inches with water. Bring water to a full boil and maintain boil for recommended time:

Fruit	Jar Size	Processing Time

Fruit	Size	Time
Apples	Pints/quarts	20 minutes
Peaches	Pints/quarts	20 minutes
Pears	Pints/quarts	20 minutes
Cherries	Pints/quarts	25 minutes
Plums	Pints/quarts	25 minutes

20 minutes, apricots, pints or quarts Altitude adjustment: Add 1 minute per 1,000 feet above 1,000 ft elevation.

6. Cooling and Storage

Remove jars carefully and place on a towel or cooling rack.

Allow to rest undisturbed for 12 to 24 hours. Check seals: lids should not flex up/down when pressed.

Remove screw bands if you prefer; store jars without bands to detect leaks.

Label jars with fruit type and canning date.

Store in a cool, dark, dry place (ideal temperature 50-70°F).

Additional Tips

Delicate fruits: If canning very delicate fruits (e.g., berries), pack loosely and add syrup carefully to avoid crushing.

Fruit floating: To reduce floating fruit, use a hot syrup and pack jars tightly without crushing.

Using juice: To reduce sweetness, you can also pack fruit in hot fruit juice rather than syrup. Sweetness preference: Adjust syrup concentration to taste or use plain water for unsweetened.

Double boiling: Some recipes recommend double boiling fruit in syrup before packing to improve texture.

Test for spoilage: If jar lid bulges, leaks, or contents smell off, discard immediately.

I can also assist you with, if you wish: Recipes for specific fruits (peaches, pears, apples, cherries, etc.)

Homemade syrup recipes using honey or alternative sweeteners

Step-by-step printable canning checklist

Chart for adjusting the height

Classic and Low-Sugar Jams

Here's a clear, easy-to-follow guide for canning Classic and Low-Sugar Jams—including key differences, basic recipes, and safe canning steps.

Canning Classic Jam vs Low-Sugar Jam: Overview

Aspect Classic Jam Low-Sugar Jam

Sugar content High (usually equal to fruit weight) Reduced sugar or uses sugar substitutes

Pectin: Natural or commercially added pectin Usually requires commercially added low-sugar pectin. Texture Thick, gelled Can be softer, needs pectin help

Preservation Utilizes more acidity, pectin, and heat than sugar, which acts as a preservative. Basic Classic Jam Recipe (Example: Strawberry)

Ingredients:

4 cups crushed fresh strawberries

4 cups granulated sugar

1/4 cup lemon juice

1 package (1.75 oz) fruit pectin (optional, depending on fruit ripeness)

Instructions:

Combine strawberries and lemon juice in a large pot.

Stir in pectin (if using), and bring to a boil over medium heat.

Add sugar all at once, stirring constantly.

Bring the mixture back to a full rolling boil and boil for 1-2 minutes.

Remove from heat and skim foam if needed.

Ladle into sterilized jars, leaving 1/4-inch headspace.

Wipe jar rims, apply lids, and screw bands fingertip-tight.

Process in boiling water bath for 10 minutes (adjust for altitude).

Take it off and let it cool on a towel-lined counter. Check seals after 24 hours.

Basic Low-Sugar Jam Recipe (Example: Blueberry)

Ingredients:

4 cups crushed blueberries

2 cups granulated sugar (or less, per pectin instructions)

14 cups juice from lemons 1.75 oz of low-sugar fruit pectin in a package Instructions:

Mix blueberries, lemon juice, and low-sugar pectin in a large pot.

Bring to a boil over medium heat, stirring frequently.

Add sugar gradually, stirring constantly.

Return to a full rolling boil and boil for 1 minute.

Skim foam after removing from heat. Ladle into sterilized jars with 1/4-inch headspace.

Apply bands and lids and wipe the rims. Process in boiling water bath for 10 minutes (adjust for altitude).

Cool the seals and check them after 24 hours. Water Bath Canning Steps (for Both):

Prepare your jars, rings, and lids (sterilize jars in the dishwasher or by boiling). Fill a large pot with water and bring it to a boil while you make jam. Fill jars with hot jam, leaving 1/4 inch headspace.

Using a damp cloth, wipe the rims clean. Apply lids and screw rings finger-tight.

Place jars on rack in boiling water bath, water covering jars by 1-2 inches.

Boil for the recommended time (usually 10 minutes).

Remove jars carefully, and place them on a towel to cool undisturbed.

After 24 hours, test seals (lid should not flex up/down).

Label jars with date and jam type.

Marmalades, Jellies, and Fruit Butters

Here's a clear, step-by-step guide for canning marmalades, jellies, and fruit butter safely and effectively. Tips for cooking, preparing, canning, and storing are included. Canning Marmalades, Jellies, and Fruit Butters

1. Preparation

Choose quality fruit: Fresh, ripe fruit without bruises or mold is best.

Wash the fruit thoroughly.

Sterilize jars and lids:

Wash jars in hot soapy water.

Jars can either be sterilized in the dishwasher or boiled in water for ten minutes. Keep jars hot until ready to fill to prevent breakage.

Simmer lids in hot (not boiling) water to soften the sealing compound.

2. Make the Marmalade/Jelly/Fruit Butter

Follow your trusted recipe carefully. Fruit juice, pulp, sugar, and pectin (for jellies and marmalades) are common ingredients. Cook the fruit mixture until it reaches the setting point:

Jellies and marmalades: should gel when tested (put a small spoonful on a cold plate, if it wrinkles when pushed, it's ready).

Fruit butter: cook until thick and smooth, without the need for gel testing.

3. Fill the Jars

Ladle the hot marmalade, jelly, or fruit butter into the sterilized jars.

Leave about 1/4 inch (6 mm) headspace.

Remove air bubbles by running a non-metallic spatula or chopstick around the inside of the jar.

Using a damp cloth, clean the rims to ensure a good seal. 4. Seal the Jars

Place the lids on jars.

Bands should be fastened with enough force to fit your fingertip. 5. Processing (Canning in a Water Bath) Use a boiling water bath canner:

Place jars on rack in canner.

Ensure jars are covered by at least 1-2 inches of water.

Bring water to a boil.

Process for the time specified by your recipe (usually 5 to 15 minutes depending on altitude and jar size).

After processing, remove the lid, turn off the heat, and let the jars sit in the water for five minutes. Remove jars and place on a towel or rack to cool undisturbed for 12-24 hours.

6. Check Seals and Store

After cooling, check seals:

The lid should be concave and not pop when pressed.

If you want, you can take off the screw bands (some people say to keep them for storage). Label jars with contents and date.

Store in a cool, dark, dry place.

Refrigerate after opening.

Tips and Notes

Use tested recipes for safety, especially with jellies and marmalades due to sugar and pectin balance.

Adjust processing times for altitude if needed (longer processing for higher altitudes).

Fruit butter typically thickens in a longer cooking time using the same water bath method. Paraffin wax should not be used for sealing because it is old and less reliable.

Pie Fillings and Compotes

A comprehensive guide to canning pie fillings and compotes covers the essentials for tasty, safe results. Canning Pie Fillings and Compotes

Typically, fruit, sugar, a thickener, and occasionally spices make up pie fillings. Compotes are fruit cooked gently with sugar, often served as a topping or dessert. Both can be preserved in cans for prolonged storage. Safety First:

Pie fillings and compotes are high-acid foods (due to fruit and sugar), so they can be safely canned using a water bath canner.

Ingredients:

Fruits like apples, berries, peaches, cherries, pears, and plums Sugar (granulated, brown, or a mix)

Thickener (flour, tapioca starch, clear Jel, or cornstarch) Lemon juice or bottled lemon juice (for acidity and color retention)

Spices (cinnamon, nutmeg, cloves - optional)

Fruit juice or water (sometimes to adjust the consistency) Basic Steps for Canning Pie Fillings or Compotes:

Fruit preparation: Wash, peel, pit, and slice the fruit as needed.

Mix Filling:

Combine fruit with sugar, spices, and lemon juice. For pie filling, add your thickener to a portion of cold water or juice first to avoid lumps, then stir it into the fruit mixture.

Cook the Mixture:

Simmer the filling gently until it thickens to the desired consistency (usually 5–10 minutes). Cook the fruit until soft but mostly intact for the compote. For pie filling, cook until thickened but still juicy.

Sterilize Jars:

Wash canning jars and lids in hot soapy water. Keep jars hot until ready to fill.

Fill Jars:

Ladle hot filling into hot jars, leaving 1-inch headspace.

Remove Air Bubbles:

Use a non-metallic spatula or chopstick to release trapped air bubbles.

Wipe Rims:

Using a damp cloth, clean the rims of the jars to ensure a good seal. Apply Lids and Rings:

Rings should be screwed into the jars with your fingertip tight. Process in Water Bath:

Process jars in a boiling water bath canner. Jars should be submerged in water for at least 12 to 18 inches. Time to Process (Water Bath Canning): Processing Time Per Jar (Minutes) Pints 25 minutes

Quarts 30 minutes

Adjust processing time for altitude as needed (add 5 minutes per 1,000 ft over 1,000 ft).

Cooling and Storing:

Remove jars and place them on a towel to cool for 12–24 hours undisturbed.

Check seals (lid should be concave and not flex when pressed).

Label jars with contents and date.

Store in a cool, dark place.

Use within 1 year for best quality.

Tips:

Use only tested recipes from reliable sources (e.g., USDA, Ball Blue Book).

Avoid thickening agents like flour or arrowroot in canned pie fillings — use cornstarch or clear Jel designed for canning.

If you want a less sweet filling, reduce sugar carefully — sugar acts as a preservative.

For compotes, keep chunks intact for texture.

If the fruit is low-acid (e.g., figs, peaches), add lemon juice to ensure safety.

Chapter 6: Canning Recipes – Vegetables & Pickles

Pickled Vegetables (Cucumbers, Beets, Carrots)

Here are simple, tested recipes for canning pickled cucumbers, beets, and carrots using a water bath canner. Each recipe includes ingredients, steps, and tips for safe preservation.

1. Classic Dill Pickled Cucumbers

Ingredients (for about 4 quarts):

8 lbs small cucumbers (pickling cucumbers)

4 cups of white vinegar with an acidity of 5% 4 cups water

1/4 cup pickling salt (or kosher salt that does not contain iodine) 8 cloves garlic (optional)

8 fresh dill heads or 4 tablespoons of dill seeds 2 teaspoons ground black pepper 2 tbsp mustard seeds

2 tsp crushed red pepper flakes (optional)

Instructions:

Wash cucumbers and trim blossom ends.

Make brine by boiling vinegar, water, and salt together. Pack cucumbers tightly into sterilized pint or quart jars. Add garlic, dill, peppercorns, mustard seeds, and red pepper flakes evenly to each jar.

Pour hot brine over cucumbers, leaving 1/2 inch headspace. Remove air bubbles.

Apply lids, wipe jar rims clean, and screw bands in place with your fingertip. Process in boiling water bath:

Pints: 10 minutes

15 minutes per gallon Then let the jars cool completely for 12 to 24 hours. Check seals before storing.

2. Pickled Beets

Ingredients (about 7 pints):

5 pounds of medium-sized beets 3 cups of white vinegar (5%)

3 mugs of water 2 mugs of sugar 1 tbsp pickling salt

1 tsp whole cloves

1 cinnamon stick per jar (optional)

1 bay leaf per jar (optional)

Instructions:

Wash beets, and trim tops leaving 1 inch of stem. Tenderize in water for about 25 to 30 minutes. Drain and remove the skins. Slice or quarter beets.

In a saucepan, combine the sugar, salt, water, and vinegar. Bring to a boil.

Pack beets into hot sterilized jars, adding cloves, cinnamon sticks, and bay leaves to each jar.

Pour hot pickling liquid over beets, leaving 1/2 inch headspace. Get rid of air bubbles. Wipe rims, and seal jars with lids and bands.

Process in boiling water bath for 30 minutes (adjust time for altitude if needed).

Let jars cool, check seals, and store in a cool dark place.

3. Carrots Pickled Ingredients (about 7 pints):

5 lbs carrots, peeled and cut into sticks or rounds

4 cups white vinegar (5%)

4 mugs of water 1/4 cup of pickling salt

Four garlic cloves (optional) 2 tbsp dill seeds or 4 heads fresh dill

2 tbsp sugar (optional, for a slightly sweet pickle)

1 tbsp whole black peppercorns

Instructions:

Wash, peel, and cut carrots. Blanch in boiling water for 2-3 minutes, then cool quickly in ice water.

Bring the water, vinegar, salt, and, if using, sugar to a boil. Pack carrots into sterilized jars, adding garlic, dill, and peppercorns evenly.

Pour hot brine over carrots, leaving 1/2 inch headspace. Remove air bubbles.

Cover jars with bands and wipe the rims clean. Process in boiling water bath for 15 minutes (adjust for altitude).

After sealing, cool and store. Tips:

Always use tested recipes and follow the correct processing times and headspace to ensure safety.

Processing times should be increased by 5 minutes if you are above 1,000 feet, and by 10 minutes if you are above 6,000 feet. Use fresh, firm vegetables for the best texture.

Store sealed jars in a cool, dark place; refrigerate after opening.

Here are a few more flavorful pickled vegetable recipes for canning, including some variations and less common veggies:

4. Cucumbers in Butter and Bread 7 pints' worth of ingredients: 6 lbs cucumbers, sliced 1/4 inch thick

5 cups of white vinegar 2 mugs of water 3 cups granulated sugar

2 tbsp pickling salt

1 tbsp mustard seeds

1 teaspoon of celery seeds 1 teaspoon turmeric powder 1 large onion, thinly sliced

Instructions:

Combine vinegar, water, sugar, salt, mustard seeds, celery seeds, and turmeric in a large pot. Bring to a boil, stirring to dissolve sugar and salt.

Layer cucumbers and onions in sterilized jars.

Pour hot brine over vegetables, leaving 1/2 inch headspace. Remove air bubbles.

Wipe rims and seal with lids and bands.

Process in boiling water bath:

10 minutes for pints 15 minutes per gallon Check the seals, cool the jars, and store. 5. Pickled Green Beans (Dilly Beans)

Ingredients (for about 7 pints):

3 lbs fresh green beans, washed and trimmed

5 cups white vinegar (5%)

5 cups water

1/4 cup pickling salt

2 tbsp dill seeds or 7 heads fresh dill

2 tbsp garlic cloves (peeled)

1 tbsp crushed red pepper flakes (optional)

Instructions:

Blanch green beans in boiling water for 2 minutes, then drain.

Bring vinegar, water, and salt to a boil.

Pack green beans vertically into jars. Add garlic, dill, and red pepper flakes evenly.

Pour hot brine over beans, leaving 1/2 inch headspace. Remove air bubbles.

Seal and process in a boiling water bath for 10 minutes.

Store, check the seals, and cool. 6. Pickled Cauliflower and Carrots Medley

Ingredients (for about 7 pints):

1 head cauliflower, cut into small florets

4 large peeled and sliced carrots 4 cups white vinegar (5%)

4 cups water

1/4 cup pickling salt

4 cloves garlic

2 tbsp mustard seeds

2 tbsp coriander seeds

1 tbsp turmeric powder

Instructions:

Carrots and cauliflower should be blanched separately for two minutes in boiling water before being cooled in ice water. Bring vinegar, water, salt, mustard seeds, coriander seeds, and turmeric to boil.

Pack vegetables into sterilized jars with garlic cloves.

Pour hot brine over vegetables, leaving 1/2 inch headspace. Remove air bubbles.

Seal jars and process in a boiling water bath for 15 minutes.

Cool and store.

7. Spicy Pickled Jalapeños

Ingredients (for about 7 pints):

3 lbs fresh jalapeños, sliced into rings

4 cups white vinegar (5%)

4 cups water

1/4 cup pickling salt

1/4 cup sugar (optional)

4 cloves garlic

2 tbsp black peppercorns

2 tbsp coriander seeds

Instructions:

Bring vinegar, water, salt, and sugar to boil.

Pack jalapeño slices and garlic cloves into sterilized jars. Add peppercorns and coriander seeds.

Pour hot brine over peppers leaving 1/2 inch headspace. Get rid of air bubbles. Seal jars and process in a boiling water bath for 10 minutes.

Cool, check seals, and store.

More Tips:

Use distilled white vinegar with 5% acidity for safe pickling.

Always keep the 1/2 inch headspace for proper sealing and processing.

Label jars with the date and contents.

Let pickled vegetables rest for at least 2 weeks before opening for the best flavor.

Relishes and Chutneys

Here's a clear, step-by-step guide to canning relishes and chutneys safely, plus some tips for success:

Canning Relishes and Chutneys: Step-by-Step Guide

1. Prepare Your Ingredients

Depending on your recipe, wash and chop fruits and vegetables. Combine ingredients in a large pot and cook according to the recipe until the relish or chutney reaches the desired consistency.

2. Sterilize Jars and Lids

Wash canning jars and lids in hot, soapy water.

Sterilize jars by boiling them for 10 minutes or keeping them hot in a simmering water bath until ready to fill.

To soften the sealing compound, place the lids in warm (but not boiling) water. 3. Complete the Jars Ladle hot relish or chutney into hot sterilized jars.

Leave 1/4-inch headspace (space between food and jar rim).

Slide a non-metallic spatula or bubble remover tool around the jar's interior to get rid of air bubbles. To ensure a tight seal, wipe the rims of the jars with a clean, damp cloth. Place lids on jars and screw bands fingertip-tight (not too tight).

4. Process in Water Bath

Place jars in a boiling water canner with at least 1-2 inches of water covering the jars.

Process jars according to your recipe's recommended time (usually 10-15 minutes for relishes and chutneys).

Start timing when water returns to a full boil.

Adjust processing times for altitude if necessary (add 1 minute per 1,000 feet above 1,000 feet).

5. Cool and Store

Remove jars carefully and place on a towel or rack to cool undisturbed for 12-24 hours.

Press the center of each lid to check for seals; it shouldn't flex up and down. Label jars with contents and date.

Keep it dry, cool, and dark. Tips for Best Results:

Use tested recipes from reliable sources like the USDA or trusted canning cookbooks to ensure safe acidity levels.

Use fresh, high-quality ingredients.

Keep jars hot until filling to prevent breakage.

Avoid overfilling jars.

The store-opened jars are in the refrigerator.

Here's a deeper dive into canning relishes and chutneys with additional details, safety tips, troubleshooting, and storage advice:

In-Depth Guide to Canning Relishes and Chutneys

What Are Relishes and Chutneys?

Relishes: Typically a finely chopped or ground mix of vegetables and/or fruits, often with vinegar, sugar, and spices. They're usually tangy and mildly spicy.

Chutneys: Can be chunkier or smooth, combining fruits, vegetables, sugar, vinegar, and spices. Chutneys can be sweet, sour, spicy, or a mix.

Why Use a Water Bath Canner?

Relishes and chutneys have high acidity (due to vinegar and sugar) which makes them safe for water bath canning.

Relishes and chutneys typically do not require pressure canning, whereas low-acid foods do. Selecting Recipes and Ingredients

Always use tested recipes from reputable sources like:

National Center for the Preservation of Homemade Foods (NCHFP) USDA Complete Guide to Home Canning

Ball Blue Book

Don't alter vinegar concentration or sugar amounts drastically; these are critical for safety.

Use fresh produce that is firm and free from blemishes.

Use the correct vinegar type (usually 5% acidity). Lower-acidity vinegars are unsafe for canning.

Preparing Your Workspace and Equipment

Clean and sanitize your work area.

Check jars for chips or cracks.

Have all your utensils and tools ready: ladles, bubble remover, jar lifter, funnel, clean towels.

Processing Times and Altitude Adjustments

Processing time depends on jar size, recipe, and altitude.

For instance, boiling the majority of relishes in pint jars takes 10 to 15 minutes. For every 1,000 feet above sea level, add 1 minute. Always adhere to the USDA guide or the recommended processing time in the recipe. Troubleshooting Common Issues

Problem Possible Cause Solution

The lid won't seal Jar rim is dirty, lid is not hot enough, and not tight enough Wipe the rim before filling, use hot lids, and tighten the bands fingertip tight

Jar breaks Jarring temperature shock, over-tightened band Keep jars hot before filling, don't tighten bands too much

Natural, cloudy liquid derived from ingredients or minerals present in the water Usually safe, but produce can be rinsed before cooking Mold or fermentation Improper sealing, recipe acidity too low Check seal; discard if mold appears, only use tested recipes

Soggy texture Overcooking or too much vinegar Follow the recipe carefully, avoid overcooking

Storage and Shelf Life

Store canned relishes and chutneys in a cool, dark place (50-70°F / 10-21°C).

Avoid direct sunlight which can degrade color and flavor.

Properly sealed jars can last 1-2 years for best quality.

Once opened, refrigerate and use within a few weeks.

Example of a Basic Canning Relish Recipe Outline

Ingredients:

4 cups chopped cucumber

2 cups chopped onion

2 cups green pepper chopped 3 cups vinegar (5%)

2 cups sugar

1/4 cup salt Spices (mustard seed, celery seed, turmeric)

Basic Methods: Combine veggies with salt; let stand for 1 hour.

Drain, rinse, and drain again.

Combine vinegar, sugar, and spices in a large pot; bring to boil.

Add vegetables; simmer 10 minutes.

Fill hot jars, leaving 1/4-inch headspace.

Process in boiling water bath for 10 minutes.

Tomatoes, Sauces, and Salsa (Water Bath and Pressure Variants)

This clear and useful guide for canning tomatoes, sauces, and salsa covers pressure canning and water bath canning, as well as important safety and acidity advice. Canning Tomatoes, Sauces, and Salsa

(Water Bath and Pressure Canning Guide)

1. Safety and preparation first Use fresh, ripe tomatoes and fresh ingredients.

Always adhere to tried-and-trusted recipes from reliable sources (such as the USDA, Ball, and National Center for Home Food Preservation). Clean jars and lids thoroughly (wash with hot soapy water and rinse well).

Keep jars hot until filling (in simmering water or dishwasher) to prevent breakage.

Every time you can use new lids. 2. Acidification (Worthwhile!) Tomatoes are borderline acid foods; to ensure safe acidity:

Add 2 tablespoons bottled lemon juice OR 1/2 teaspoon citric acid per quart jar (1 tablespoon lemon juice or 1/4 tsp citric acid per pint jar).

This prevents bacterial growth and ensures safety in water bath canning.

3. Preparing Tomatoes and Sauces

Peel tomatoes by blanching (dipping in boiling water for 30 to 60 seconds, then cooling in ice water) for whole or halved tomatoes. For Sauces and Salsa: Prepare as per recipe, cooking to desired consistency and adding vinegar or lemon juice to adjust acidity as needed.

4. Water Bath Canning (High-Acid Foods)

Used for:

Whole peeled tomatoes (acidified)

Tomato sauces with added lemon juice or vinegar

Salsas with enough acid (vinegar or lemon juice) and no low-acid ingredients

Steps:

Fill jars leaving 1/2-inch headspace.

Using a spatula that is not made of metal, remove air bubbles. Wipe rims clean, apply lids and screw bands fingertip-tight.

Place jars in boiling water bath (water should cover jars by 1-2 inches).

Process:

Tomatoes (whole or crushed): ~40-85 minutes depending on altitude and jar size.

Tomato sauce/salsa: 15-85 minutes depending on recipe and jar size.

Carefully remove the jars and let them cool on a towel or rack. After 12-24 hours, check the seals (lid should not flex when pressed).

5. Canning under pressure (for thick or low-acid sauces) Make use of pressure canners for: Sauces made with thick tomatoes and no acid Unless additional acid is added, salsa with low-acid ingredients like onions and peppers Tomatoes either whole or crushed (pressure-canning allows for acid-free canning) Steps:

Prepare jars as above.

Fill the pressure canner with 2-3 inches of water.

Place jars on a rack inside the canner.

Lock the lid and heat to vent steam for 10 minutes.

Close the vent and build pressure to 10-15 psi (depending on altitude).

Process:

Tomatoes: 20-25 minutes for pints, 25-30 minutes for quarts at 10 psi (adjust pressure for altitude).

Sauces and salsas: 20-30 minutes depending on the recipe.

Cool the pressure canner naturally before removing the lid and jars.

Remove jars and cool on a towel. Check seals after 12-24 hours.

6. Adjusting for Altitude

Increase processing time or pressure for altitudes above 1,000 feet:

Water bath: add 5-10 minutes of processing time for every 1,000 feet above sea level.

Pressure canning: increase pressure to 15 psi for altitudes above 1,000 feet (check your canner manual).

7. Storage Tips

Label jars with date and contents.

Store in a cool, dark, dry place.

Use within 1 year for best quality.

Before using, check the seals. Let me expand the guide with deeper details, plus common recipes, troubleshooting, and safety reminders for tomatoes, sauces, and salsa canning.

Expanded Guide: Canning Tomatoes, Sauces & Salsa

8. Detailed Preparation Tips

Peeling Tomatoes

Blanch and shock: Bring water to a boil, dip tomatoes in it for 30 to 60 seconds until the skins split, and then plunge them into ice water. Skins slip right off.

Core first: Remove stem scar before blanching to make peeling easier.

Preparing Tomato Sauce

Cook tomatoes down to the desired thickness.

Season with salt, herbs, spices, onions, and peppers (check the recipe for acid level).

Add acid (lemon juice or vinegar) for safety.

Preparing Salsa

Chop vegetables uniformly.

Add vinegar/lemon juice to ensure acidity pH <4.6.

Adjust seasonings to taste (cilantro, garlic, onions, jalapeños, etc.).

9. Recipes & Processing Times

A. Whole or Halved Tomatoes (Water Bath)

Add lemon juice or citric acid.

Processing Time:

Pints: 35-40 minutes

Quarts: 45-50 minutes

B. Sauce made with tomatoes Acidify with lemon juice or vinegar.

Processing Time:

Pints: 35 minutes

Quarts: 40 minutes

C. Salsa (Water Bath)

Must have enough vinegar/lemon juice to be acidic.

Processing Time:

Pints: 15-20 minutes

Quarts: 20-25 minutes

D. Pressure Canning Tomatoes and Sauces

No acidification is needed if pressure canning whole or crushed tomatoes.

Time taken to process: Pints: 20 minutes

Quarts: 25 minutes

Pressure: 10 to 15 psi, depending on the elevation.

10. Troubleshooting Common Issues

Problem Possible Cause Solution

The jar seal failed Improper jar rim cleaning; lid old Wipe rim clean; use new lids each time

Tomatoes float or discolor Air bubbles or oxidation Remove air bubbles; use an acidifier

Too thin or not sufficiently cooked before canning? Cook the sauce longer to thicken it. Soggy salsa or soft veggies Over-processing or wrong recipe Follow tested recipes; avoid long cooking

11. Safety & Best Practices

Always acidify tomatoes for water bath canning.

Use tested recipes, especially for salsa. Ingredients and acidity must be balanced for safety.

Use a pressure canner for low-acid sauces or salsas.

Never alter ingredient ratios without consulting tested sources.

Check seals before storage; discard jars with bulging lids, leaks, or off-smells.

12. Step-by-Step Printable Checklist Sample

Would you like me to prepare a printable checklist for either a water bath or pressure canning of tomatoes, sauces, or salsa? This can help ensure nothing gets missed in the process.

If you want, I can also include:

Tips on adjusting recipes for altitude and equipment.

How to label and track batches so they can be stored and rotated optimally. Tips for troubleshooting spoilage or safety concerns.

Green Beans, Corn, and Mixed Vegetables (Pressure Canning)

Pressure canning is essential for safely preserving low-acid vegetables like green beans, corn, and mixed vegetables. Here's a step-by-step guide for each, followed by a general checklist you can print and use for batch tracking.

Guide for Pressure Canning Everything Else: Canner under pressure Rings and lids for pint and quart canning jars Jar lifter, funnel, bubble remover tool

Clean cloths or paper towels

Optional salt: 12 teaspoons per pint, 1 teaspoon per quart Boiling water (or broth)

1. Green beans, either in a hot pack or raw, Prep:

Wash, snap ends, and cut into 1–2" pieces.

Recommended: Boil a hot pack for five minutes. Packing:

Pack into jars, leaving a headspace of one inch. If you like, add salt. Fill with boiling water, remove bubbles, and adjust headspace.

Time to complete: Pressure (Dial Gauge: 0–2,000 ft) and Time in the Jar Pints 11 lbs 20 min

Quarts 11 lbs 25 min

(For the weighted gauge, use 10 pounds; adjust for altitude if necessary.) 2. Corn (Whole Kernel, Hot Pack Only)

Prep:

Husk, silk, and blanch cobs for 3 minutes.

Cut kernels from cob (do not scrape cob).

Packing:

Hot pack only: Boil kernels in water for 5 minutes.

Pack into jars with 1-inch headspace.

Add salt if desired.

Fill with cooking water, remove bubbles, and adjust headspace.

Process Times:

Jar Size Pressure (Dial Gauge: 0–2,000 ft) Time

Pints 11 lbs 55 min

11 quarts, 85 min. 3. Mixed Vegetables (No Tomatoes)

Suggested Mix: Carrots, corn, green beans, peas, lima beans (avoid starchy or dry beans unless pre-soaked and cooked).

Prep:

Wash, peel (if needed), and dice all vegetables.

Blanch each type one at a time for two to three minutes. Packing:

Mix veggies evenly.

Hot pack: Boil mix in water for 5 minutes.

Pack into jars with 1-inch headspace.

Add salt if desired.

Remove any bubbles and adjust the headspace after filling with hot water. Process Times:

Jar Size Pressure (Dial Gauge: 0–2,000 ft) Time

Pints 11 lbs 75 min

Quarts 11 lbs 90 min

Checklist for Pressure Canning Vegetables— Printable Before You Proceed: Inspect jars and lids for cracks/chips.

Wash and sanitize jars, lids, and rings.

Prepare the pressure canner and examine the gasket and vent pipe. If using non-self-sealing lids, boil water for hot packs and lids. Prep Vegetables:

Wash and trim/peel as needed.

Depending on the recipe, blanch or precook. Add salt if desired. Filling Jars:

Use a funnel to fill jars.

Leave 1-inch headspace.

Get rid of air bubbles. With a damp cloth, wipe the rims. Finger-tightly apply the lids and screw bands. Processing:

In a canner, fill the jars with 2 to 3 inches of hot water. Shut the lid and let the steam out for ten minutes. Apply weight or close the vent.

Execute at the appropriate pressure and time. Turn off the heat and let the pressure naturally fall back to zero. After ten minutes, lift the lid away from the face.
After Processing:

Use a jar lifter to remove jars.

Place on a towel, undisturbed, for 12–24 hours.

Verify seals. Remove rings. Wipe jars.

Label with date, batch, and contents.

Store in a cool, dark place.

Chapter 7: Canning Recipes – Meats & Meals

Canning Poultry, Beef, and Pork

Pressure canning is used to preserve poultry, beef, and pork, not water bath canning because these low-acid foods require high temperatures to prevent botulism and other harmful bacteria. A comprehensive guide to pressure canning meat safely includes general instructions, USDA-approved processing times, and success strategies. Pressure Canning Poultry, Beef, and Pork (Chunks, Strips, or Cubes)

You'll Need:

Pressure canner (NOT a pressure cooker)

Canning jars (pint or quart), lids, and rings

Jar lifter, funnel, and debubbler

Boiling water or broth (for hot pack)

Optional salt: 1 teaspoon per quart, 12 teaspoons per pint Detailed Instructions 1. Prepare the Meat

You can use either the raw pack or hot pack method:

Raw Pack (Easiest)

Reduce excess fat. Cut meat into cubes or strips (leave bones in for bone-in meats if desired).

Pack raw meat into jars, leaving 1-inch headspace.

Do not add liquid—meat makes its juices during canning.

Hot Pack (Better for Quality)

Lightly brown or pre-cooked meat until rare.

Put the hot meat in jars. Add hot broth, water, or meat juices, leaving 1-inch headspace.

Optional: Add salt for flavor (not preservation).

2. Prepare Jars and Lids

Wash jars, lids, and rings in hot soapy water.

Keep jars warm until ready to use.

Lids: Follow the manufacturer's directions (some no longer require pre-warming).

3. Remove Air Bubbles and Wipe Rims

Use a plastic tool to release air bubbles.

Wipe jar rims with vinegar-dampened cloth to ensure a clean seal.

Screw the lids on with fingertip tightness. 4. Load the Pressure Canner

Check the manual for your canner to determine how much water to add to the canner. Place jars inside the canner using a jar lifter.

Secure the lid and begin heating.

5. Vent the Canner

To remove air, allow steam to vent for ten minutes. After venting, add the weight or close the petcock.

6. Process the Jars

Use the chart below for processing times and pressures.

Meat Type Jar Size Process Time Pressure

Pints of poultry (boneless or bone-in) 75 minutes 10 lbs (dial) / 11 lbs (weighted) Poultry (boneless or bone-in) Quarts 90 min 10 lbs (dial) / 11 lbs (weighted)

Beef or Pork (chunks/strips) Pints 75 min 10 lbs (dial) / 11 lbs (weighted)

Beef or Pork (chunks/strips) Quarts 90 min 10 lbs (dial) / 11 lbs (weighted)

IMPORTANT: Adjust pressure for altitude:

0–1,000 ft: 10 lbs (dial) / 11 lbs (weighted)

1,001–2,000 ft: 11 lbs (dial) / 15 lbs (weighted)

2,001–4,000 ft: 12 lbs (dial) / 15 lbs (weighted)

4,001–6,000 ft: 13 lbs (dial) / 15 lbs (weighted)

6,001–8,000 ft: 14 lbs (dial) / 15 lbs (weighted)

7. Cool and Check Seals

Let the canner cool naturally. Do not force the pressure release.

Remove jars and let cool for 12–24 hours.

Check seals: the lids should not flex when pressed.

Wash, label, and store jars in a cool, dark place.

Storage Tips

Store in a pantry at 50–70°F.

Best used within 12 to 18 months, but can last longer if seals are still intact. Always inspect for signs of spoilage before use.

Soups, Stews, and Chili

Canning soups, stews, and chili can be a great way to preserve hearty meals, but because these are low-acid foods, they must be pressure-canned to be safe from botulism. A comprehensive guide to safe pressure canning is provided here, with a printable checklist at the end. General Rules for Canning Soups, Stews, and Chili

Pressure Canner Required – No exceptions.

No Dairy, Flour, Pasta, or Thickeners – Add these when reheating.

Use Precooked Beans Only – If your recipe includes beans.

Avoid rice and barley because they expand too much and could compromise safety. Only Use Tested Recipes – Modify with care, especially with meats.

Basic Steps for Pressure Canning Soup or Chili

Ingredients Prep

Use fully cooked meats and pre-soaked or fully cooked beans.

Lightly cook vegetables before canning for the best texture.

Make use of a tomato base or broth with no additional thickeners. Leave room for expansion—fill jars only 2/3 with solids, then add broth.

Jar Filling

Sterilize jars (especially for longer process times).

Fill hot jars with hot soup/stew/chili, leaving 1-inch headspace.

Remove air bubbles with a spatula.

Apply the rings and lids finger-tight after wiping the rims with vinegar. Pressure Canning Process

Add 2–3 inches of water to the pressure canner.

Load jars into canner.

Shut the lid and let the steam out for ten minutes. Increase pressure to: 10 lbs for weighted gauge canner (at sea level)

11 lbs for dial gauge canner (at sea level)

Adjust for elevation (see the table below) Process Times:

Pints: 60 minutes

Quarts: 75–90 minutes (depends on density; chili and thick stews often 90 min)

Turn off the heat and let the pressure naturally fall back to zero. Wait 10 minutes before opening the lid.

Cool the jars for 12 to 24 hours. Adjustments to the altitude for pressure canning Altitude Dial Gauge Weighted Gauge

0–1,000 ft 11 lbs 10 lbs

1,001–2,000 ft 11 lbs 15 lbs

2,001–4,000 ft 12 lbs 15 lbs

4,001–6,000 ft 13 lbs 15 lbs

6,001–8,000 ft 14 lbs 15 lbs

Printable Checklist for Canning Soups, Stews & Chili

[ ] Gather ingredients – no dairy, thickeners, or grains

[ ] Precook meats and beans

[ ] Lightly cook vegetables

[ ] Heat broth or tomato base

[Sterilize the jars] [ ] Fill jars (2/3 solids, then liquid)

[ ] Leave 1-inch headspace

[ ] Debubble and wipe rims

[ ] Apply lids and rings

[ ] Add 2–3" water to pressure canner

[ ] Load jars into canner

[Let the steam escape for ten minutes]. [ ] Bring to correct pressure for your altitude

[ ] Process:

Pints – 60 minutes

Quarts – 75–90 minutes

[ ] Allow pressure to return to zero

[ ] Cool jars 12–24 hours

[ ] Check seals, label, and store

Beans and Legumes

Home canning of beans and legumes is a great way to have ready-to-use, convenient protein at any time. However, because they are low-acid foods and carry the risk of botulism if not properly processed, they must be pressure canned rather than water bath canned. A complete guide to pressure canning beans and legumes, such as black beans, pinto beans, kidney beans, and chickpeas, is provided here. Step-by-Step: Pressure Canning Beans & Legumes

Materials You'll Need: Canner under pressure (not a pressure cooker) pint or quart canning jars Rings and lids (each time, new lids) Jar lifter, canning funnel, bubble remover

Large bowl, pot, or strainer for beans

Clean cloth or paper towels

Ingredients:

Dried beans or legumes (approx. ¾ cup dried = 1 pint jar; 1½ cups = 1 quart)

Water

Optional: salt (½ tsp per pint, 1 tsp per quart)

Instructions:

1. Sort beans and rinse them. Pick through beans to remove debris or damaged ones.

Rinse thoroughly in cold water.

2. Soak Beans

Overnight Soak: Cover the beans in a large pot with water and let them soak for 12 to 18 hours. Quick Soak (faster method): Cover beans with water, bring to a boil for 2 minutes, turn off heat, and let sit for 1 hour.

3. Parboil Beans

After soaking, drain and rinse beans.

Add fresh water, bring to a boil, and simmer for 30 minutes. This partially cooks them and prevents expansion in jars.

4. Prepare Jars and Lids

Wash jars in hot, soapy water or run through dishwasher.

Heat lids in simmering (not boiling) water if using metal lids.

5. Empty Jars Fill hot jars with parboiled beans using a canning funnel.

Add hot cooking liquid or fresh boiling water to cover beans, leaving 1 inch headspace.

Add salt if desired.

Remove bubbles and adjust headspace.

Wipe rims clean, place lids on, and screw on bands fingertip-tight.

6. Pressure Can

Place jars in pressure canner with 2–3 inches of simmering water.

Lock lid, vent steam for 10 minutes, then bring to pressure:

Pint jars: 75 minutes

Quart jars: 90 minutes

Use the appropriate pressure for your canner type and altitude:

Altitude	Dial-Gauge Pressure	Weighted-Gauge Pressure
0–1,000 ft	11 lbs	10 lbs
1,001–2,000 feet	11 pounds	15 pounds
2,001–4,000 ft	12 lbs	15 lbs
4,001–6,000 ft	13 lbs	15 lbs
6,001–8,000 ft	14 lbs	15 lbs

7. Cool and Store

After processing, turn off heat. Before opening, allow the canner to completely depressurize. Remove jars and let cool on a towel for 12–24 hours.

Check seals, remove bands, and label jars with date and contents.

Store in a cool, dark place.

Safety Tips

Because dry beans expand and can prevent proper sealing, you should never skip the steps of soaking and boiling. Always use tested pressure canning methods for legumes—never water bath.

Reprocess within 24 hours or refrigerate and use within 3–5 days if a jar does not seal.

Bone Broth and Stocks

Canning bone broth and stocks is a fantastic way to preserve nutrient-dense, homemade liquids for soups, stews, and more. Because broth is a low-acid food, it must be pressure-canned to ensure safety.

Here's a detailed step-by-step guide for pressure canning bone broth or stock, followed by a printable checklist.

How to Pressure Can Bone Broth or Stock

Tools & Equipment

Canner that uses pressure rather than a water bath
Canning jars (pint or quart)

Lids and bands

Jar lifter

Funnel

Ladle

cheesecloth or a strainer with a fine mesh Large pot for broth

Detailed Instructions 1. Make and Prepare Your Broth

Simmer bones (chicken, beef, etc.) with vegetables and herbs for 12–24 hours.

Let cool slightly, then strain the broth through a fine mesh strainer or cheesecloth.

Let sit in the fridge (if desired) to skim off solidified fat for clearer broth (optional but recommended).

Reheat broth to a simmer before canning (hot pack method).

2. Prepare the lids and jars. Wash jars, lids, and bands in hot soapy water.

Keep jars hot until ready to use (in hot water or a low oven).

Heat lids if recommended by the manufacturer.

3. Complete the Jars Using a funnel, ladle hot broth into hot jars.

Leave 1-inch headspace.

Remove air bubbles (with a bubble remover or knife).

Wipe jar rims with vinegar-dampened cloth to remove any residue.

Apply lids and screw-on bands to the fingertip tight.

4. Load Pressure Canner

Add the recommended amount of water (usually 2–3 inches) to the canner.

Place jars on the rack inside the canner.

Lock the lid in place.

5. Pressurize and Vent Heat on high until steam vents steadily for 10 minutes.

Then close the vent or add weight to begin pressurizing.

6. Make use of jars Process at the pressure recommended for your altitude:

Jar Size Pressure (0–1,000 ft) Process Time

Pints 10 lbs (dial) / 11 lbs (weighted) 20 minutes

25 minutes, quarts, 10 pounds (dial) / 11 pounds (weighted). Adjust pressure for altitude:

Dial gauge: add 1 lb per 2,000 ft above sea level.

Weighted gauge: increase to 15 lbs above 1,000 ft.

7. Cool and Store

Turn off the heat and let the canner return to zero pressure naturally.

Wait 10 more minutes before removing the lid.

Remove jars and place on a towel-lined surface.

Let cool for 12–24 hours. Check seals.

Label and store in a cool, dark place for up to 1 year.

Printable Checklist – Canning Bone Broth or Stock

Preparation

Simmer bones with vegetables/herbs for 12–24 hours.

Strain broth; refrigerate if skimming fat.

Reheat broth to a simmer.

Jars and Equipment

Wash jars, lids, and bands.

Keep jars hot until filling.

Heat lids (if needed).

Filling Jars

Ladle hot broth into jars (1-inch headspace).

Remove air bubbles.

Use vinegar to clean the rims. Apply lids and bands (fingertip tight).

Pressure Canning

Add water to the canner.

Load jars onto the rack.

Lock the lid and vent the steam for 10 minutes.

Add weight or close the vent.

Processing

Process pints (20 min) or quarts (25 min).

Adjust pressure to account for altitude. After Canning

Let the pressure naturally fall to zero. Wait 10 min, then open the lid.

Remove jars; cool for 12–24 hours.

Check seals.

Label and store.

Chapter 8:
Troubleshooting & Tips

Identifying Seal Failures

Identifying seal failures in canning is crucial to ensure food safety and prevent spoilage or botulism. Here's how to recognize a failed seal, both immediately after processing and during storage:

Within Minutes of Processing Check these once the jars are completely cool (12–24 hours after processing):

The lid neither "pops" nor curves inward. A properly sealed lid is concave (slightly curved downward) and does not flex when pressed in the center.

The jar did not seal if it popped up and down or clicked. Lid Comes Off Easily

The lid ought to be securely fastened to the jar when the ring band is removed. The seal failed if it lifted off without resistance. During processing, the jar bursts. Food or liquid on the outside of the jar, or in the canner water, may mean the jar siphoned and didn't seal properly.

Under the Lid, Seepage, or Bubbling Any bubbling or seepage under the lid after cooling is an indication of a compromised seal. During Transport Even sealed jars can lose their seal later. Check for these signs:

Bulging Covers A serious warning is a lid that is domed or bulging. Do not open or consume—dispose of the contents safely.

Rust or Corrosion

Rust under the lid or ring can eat through the seal and allow air in.

Unusual Odors

Upon opening, any foul, sour, or off smell means the food is spoiled—even if the seal seemed intact.

Mold or Discoloration

Visible mold, cloudiness in the liquid, or change in color/texture are signs of spoilage.

Seal Released

If a jar that was sealed once has a loose lid or pops when pressed, it has become unsealed over time. What to Do with Unsealed Jars

Within 24 hours of processing: Reprocess with a new lid or refrigerate and use within a few days.

After 24 hours or if signs of spoilage are present: Do not reprocess or taste. Discard the contents safely.

Reprocessing Guidelines

Reprocessing Guidelines in Canning refers to the safe methods for re-canning jars when a processing error or sealing failure has occurred. Here's a clear, printable-style summary:

Reprocessing Guidelines for Home Canning

When to Reprocess

Reprocessing is only safe if done within 24 hours of the original canning attempt. Reprocess if:

A jar did not seal.

You forgot to remove air bubbles.

The processing time or pressure was incorrect.

During cooling, the lid was bumped and unsealed. You omitted an ingredient that doesn't affect safety, like a seasoning, by accident. Do NOT Reprocess If

Since the first canning, more than a day has passed. The food has a foul odor, discoloration, or signs of spoilage. Without the appropriate amount of time or pressure, low-acid food (vegetables, meat, beans, etc.) was processed. You want to reprocess a second time (only safe once).

How to Reprocess Properly

Remove Lid: Open the jar and discard the lid.

Adjust headspace in accordance with the recipe's recommendations. Wipe Rim: Ensure the rim is clean and undamaged.

Use a New Lid: Always use a new lid. Rings can be reused.

Reprocess:

Water Bath: Make use of the entire initial processing time. Use the original time and pressure for the particular food and jar size in the pressure canner. Cool and Check Seal: Perform the usual checks for sealing after processing. Alternatives to Reprocessing

If you don't want to reprocess:

Use the unsealed jar within a few days of refrigeration. Freeze the contents in a freezer-safe container (leave headspace for expansion).

Tips

Label reprocessed jars clearly with the date and a note that they were reprocessed.

Use reprocessed jars sooner, as quality may decline.

Storage and Shelf Life

Here's an overview of storage and shelf life in canning, including best practices to ensure safety and quality:

Storage Guidelines for Canned Goods

1. Ideal Storage Conditions

Cool temperature: 50°F to 70°F (10°C to 21°C) is optimal.

Dark location: Keep jars away from direct sunlight to preserve color, nutrients, and flavor.

Dry area: To prevent lids and rings from rusting, avoid damp environments. 2. Proper Placement

Store jars upright (do not stack without a barrier like cardboard between layers).

After the jars have been sealed and cooled, remove the rings to prevent moisture from being trapped, which can lead to rust or false seals. Label each jar with contents and date.

Foods canned at home last longer Type of Food Recommended Shelf Life Notes

High-acid foods (e.g. jams, pickles, tomatoes with added acid) 12–18 months May retain quality longer if stored properly.

Low-acid foods (e.g. meats, vegetables, beans) 12 months Must be pressure canned. For the best quality, use within one year. Fruit preserves and syrups Up to 18 months Sugar helps with longer shelf stability.

Tomato products (with acid added) 12–18 months Acidity helps preserve quality.

Note: These timelines refer to quality, not safety. The food is safe for as long as the seal is intact, but its texture, flavor, and nutritional value may decrease. Signs of Spoilage (Do NOT Use if Any of These Are Present):

Seal/lid that is missing or bulging rusting or leaking from the lid Off smell or discoloration

Mold inside the jar

Bubbles or fizzing when opened (not due to fermentation)

Unusual texture or sliminess

Tips for Quick Storage Rotate stock using FIFO (First In, First Out).

Inspect jars every few months for seal integrity and spoilage.

Keep a storage log to track batches and estimate when they will expire.

Common Questions Answered

Here are some frequently asked canning questions and their concise and useful responses. These apply primarily to water baths and pressure canning, which are the two main home canning methods.

General Canning Questions

1. What distinguishes pressure canning from water bath canning? Water bath canning is for high-acid foods (like fruits, pickles, and jams).

Pressure canning is for low-acid foods (like vegetables, meats, soups) to prevent botulism.

2. Before canning, do I need to sterilize the jars? If processing time is 10 minutes or more, sterilization is not required—just clean and hot jars.

For under 10 minutes, jars must be sterilized first.

3. How long do home-canned goods last?

Best quality: 1 year.

Safe for consumption: Up to 18 months or longer if properly sealed and stored. 4. Can I reuse canning lids?

No. Use new lids each time to ensure a proper seal.

If they're in good condition, jars and rings can be used again. 5. Why did my jars not seal?

Common reasons:

Not enough headspace

Damaged jar rim or lid

Not wiped clean before sealing

Lid not centered

Not processed long enough

You can reprocess within 24 hours or refrigerate and use within a few days.

Canning in a Water Bath Specific 6. Can I water bath can vegetables or meat?

No. These are low-acid foods and must be pressure-canned to avoid botulism.

7. Can I adjust recipes to use less sugar or vinegar?

Be careful: Changing acidity can make food unsafe. Only use tested recipes if adjusting ingredients.

8. What does "headspace" mean?

Between the food and the lid is the space. The jar may not seal if there is too much. If there isn't enough, food could leak out and break the seal. Pressure Canning Specific

9. How do I know if I need to adjust for altitude?

If you're above 1,000 ft, you need to increase processing pressure or time depending on your method.

10. How do I know my pressure canner reached the right pressure?

Depending on the kind, use the gauge or the weight. Only start the timer once the correct pressure is reached and maintained.

Storage and Security 11. How should I store my canned goods?

Cool, dark place (50–70°F)

No direct sunlight or heat sources

Label with date

12. How can I tell if home-canned food has gone bad?

Mold, bubbling lids, leaks, off odors, or bubbling. When in doubt, throw it out—do not taste it!

13. Can I reuse jars from store-bought foods?

No. These are not designed for home canning and may break or not seal properly.

Chapter 9: Creative Canning & Gifting

Unique Flavor Combinations

Unique flavor combinations in canning can elevate your preserved goods, making them exciting and memorable. Here are some creative ideas that blend unexpected ingredients or flavor profiles for jams, pickles, salsas, sauces, and more:

Unique Canning Flavor Combinations 1. Sweet and sour preserves and jams Peach, Jalapeno, and Mint are juicy peaches that have a spicy kick and a finish of fresh mint. Strawberry + Black Pepper + Balsamic Vinegar — sweet berries balanced with pepper heat and tangy balsamic

Mango + Habanero + Lime — tropical sweetness with fiery heat and citrus brightness

2. Savory Pickles with a Twist

Cucumber, dill, garlic, and horseradish make these classic dill pickles extra spicy. Beets, orange peel, and cloves are earthy beets flavored with citrus and spice. Green Beans + Mustard Seeds + Curry Powder — vibrant pickled beans with a curry flair

3. Salsas & Relishes with Unexpected Notes

A smoky, sweet, and tangy tropical salsa made with tomatoes, roasted corn, chili, and pineapple. Cucumber + Watermelon + Mint + Lime — refreshing, slightly sweet salsa perfect for summer

Peach + Red Onion + Jalapeño + Thyme — sweet and spicy fruit salsa with herbal depth

4. Chutneys and sauces with complex flavors Apple + Ginger + Tamarind — sweet-tart chutney with warm spice and tangy tamarind

Sauce made with tomato, roasted red pepper, ancho chili, and cocoa powder is smoky and rich with a hint of chocolate. Plum + Star Anise + Cinnamon + Cardamom — fragrant chutney with deep warm spice notes

5. Fruit-specific spreads and butters Pear + Vanilla + Cardamom — smooth, aromatic butter with warm spice

Fig + Black Walnut + Port Wine — rich, nutty, and fruity spread with a hint of wine

Pumpkin + Maple + Nutmeg + Cayenne — autumnal flavor with a slight spicy kick

Labeling and Decorating Jars

Labeling and decorating jars in canning is a great way to make your preserves look beautiful and organized, whether for gifts, personal use, or selling. A straightforward guide with suggestions and ideas is provided here: Labeling Canning Jars

Important Information to Include: Name of the product (e.g., Strawberry Jam, Dill Pickles)

Date canned (month/year or full date)

Ingredients (optional but helpful, especially for gifts or selling)

Special inscriptions, such as "Low Sugar," "Spicy," and "Family Recipe," Label Materials:

Printable adhesive labels (waterproof or water-resistant recommended)

Tags made of kraft paper and tied with ribbon or twine Chalkboard labels or stickers for reusable jars

Washi tape with handwritten notes

Where the Label Goes: Front of the jar for product name and date

Top lid with a date or batch number (very small and private) Back or side for ingredients or notes

Label Design Tips:

Use fonts that are easy to read. Add decorative elements like borders, small fruit or vegetable icons, or floral motifs

Choose hues that go well with the contents of the jar, like red for strawberry jam. How to Decorate Canning Jars Lid Covers:

Cut fabric circles (cotton, gingham, or burlap) larger than the lid

Place fabric over the lid, secure it with a rubber band or ribbon, then screw on the ring

Great for rustic or vintage-style gifts

Ribbon and Twine:

Wrap around the neck of the jar

Labels or small charms such as dried flowers, wooden spoons, and tiny wooden tags Tags:

Use cardstock or craft paper tags

Punch a hole and tie with twine or ribbon around the jar neck

Painted Jars:

Write directly on jars or lids with paint markers made of glass. Create designs that are themed or seasonal (such as pumpkins for the fall and snowflakes for the winter). Stickers and Washi Tape:

Apply themed stickers or decorative tape for a quick and colorful finish

Pro Advice If jars will be refrigerated or frozen after opening, waterproof or laminated labels work best.

For long-term storage, keep labels simple and clear to avoid confusion.

Always let the jars cool completely before labeling, to prevent condensation from ruining the label.

Store labeled jars upright in a cool, dark place for the best shelf life.

Creating Gift Sets and Seasonal Baskets

Creating gift sets and seasonal baskets with canned goods is a fantastic way to share homemade treats and add a personal touch to your gifts! Here is a comprehensive guide to making seasonal baskets and beautiful canned gift sets: Step 1: Select Your Event and Theme Holidays (Christmas, Thanksgiving), Easter, picnics in the summer, harvests in the fall, and so on are examples of seasonal themes. Examples of gift sets: Jam and Jelly Sets

Pickles and Ferments Sets

Sauce and Salsa Selections Chutney and Relish Assortments

Soup or Stew Mixes in jars

Breakfast sets (fruit preserves, honey, pancake syrup)

Step 2: Select and Prepare Your Canned Goods

Use your favorite tested recipes for jams, pickles, sauces, etc.

Consider color variety and flavors to create an appealing mix.

Make sure all jars are properly sealed and labeled with ingredients, date, and expiration.

Step 3: Choose Your Containers and Presentation

Containers:

Decorative baskets or wooden crates

Fabric totes or reusable boxes Large gift bags or rustic trays

Packaging materials:

For cushioning, use straw, shredded tissue, or crinkle paper. Cellophane wrap or clear bags for individual jars

Ribbon, twine, or seasonal greenery for decoration

Labels & tags:

Handmade or printed gift tags with the jar contents and any special notes

Add "Made with Love" or holiday greetings

Step 4: Assemble the Basket

Place heavier jars at the bottom and lighter ones on top.

Use filler material to secure jars and prevent shifting.

Arrange jars aesthetically by size and color.

Optional additions of complementary items: Small kitchen tools (wooden spoons, spreaders)

Tea bags, coffee packets, or baked goods

Fresh herbs or dried flowers for a seasonal touch

Step 5: Final Touches

Wrap the entire basket in cellophane or decorative wrap if desired.

Tie a big ribbon or bow on top.

Include a personalized note or recipe card using one of the canned goods.

Bonus Tips:

Matching flavors: Pair jams with crackers or cheese in the basket.

Dietary preferences: Make sugar-free, vegan, or allergy-friendly jars for specific recipients.

Label clarity: Include allergen info and storage instructions on labels.

Shelf life: Inform recipients of the gift's best-before date and how to store it after it has been opened.

Printed in Dunstable, United Kingdom